MURDERED ON DUTY

SECOND EDITION

MURDERED ON DUTY

The Killing of Police Officers in America

By

SAMUEL G. CHAPMAN

Professor Emeritus
University of Oklahoma
Norman, Oklahoma

With a Foreword by

Charles Remsberg

Calibre Press
Northbrook, Illinois

CHARLES C THOMAS • PUBLISHER, LTD.
Springfield • Illinois • U.S.A.

0024896

Published and Distributed Throughout the World by
CHARLES C THOMAS • PUBLISHER, LTD.
2600 South First Street
Springfield, Illinois 62794-9265

This book is protected by copyright. No part of
it may be reproduced in any manner without
written permission from the publisher

© *1998 by* CHARLES C THOMAS • PUBLISHER, LTD.
ISBN 0-398-06820-8 (cloth)
ISBN 0-398-06821-6 (paper)
Library of Congress Catalog Card Number: 97-30462

With THOMAS BOOKS *careful attention is given to all details of manufacturing and design. It is the Publisher's desire to present books that are satisfactory as to their physical qualities and artistic possibilities and appropriate for their particular use.* THOMAS BOOKS *will be true to those laws of quality that assure a good name and good will.*

Printed in the United States of America
CR-R-3

Library of Congress Cataloging in Publication Data

Chapman, Samuel G.
    Murdered on duty : the killing of police officers in
America / by Samual G. Chapman ; with a foreword by
Charles Remsberg. -- 2nd ed.
      p.   cm.
    Rev. ed. of: Cops, killers, and staying alive.
    Includes bibliographical references and index.
    ISBN 0-398-06820-8 (cloth). -- ISBN 0-398-06821-6 (paper)
    1. Police murders--United States. 2. Police murders-
Oklahoma. 3. Police murders--United States--Prevention.
I. Chapman, Samuel G. Cops, killers, and staying alive. II. Title.
HV8138.C52   1997
364. 15' 23' 0883632--dc21   97-30462
                                                                CIP

FOREWORD

America's police enjoy no immunity from violence, as about 70 have been murdered on duty each year so far this decade. Another 70,000 have been assaulted annually, but without a fatal consequence. These numbers, while large, do not make law enforcement the nation's most deadly occupation: that dubious distinction belongs to cab drivers. Nevertheless, the amount of violence against police is troublesome, and begs for attention.

There is something very special about a fatal attack on an officer. Of course, it is a sad event, with a dramatic farewell, akin almost to the pomp of the passing of a President. Officers gather from scores of police departments, and stand at somber attention in full dress uniform. A file of squad cars, with emergency lights flashing, winds its way to the horizon in the cortege. The bagpipe wail of *Amazing Grace* is heard as the tearful widow and kids are presented an American flag, folded with military precision, as parents look on.

The service conveys a strong symbolic impact beyond the sadness and ceremony. Here was a man or woman who volunteered for the dirty, but necessary, job of dealing with people the rest of us don't want to—or can't—deal with, and then paid for that effort with his or her life. When an officer is attacked, the fragile barrier between "us" and "them" is strained. We sense, correctly, that the forces of evil who would take on a cop, a person bearing the legal authority and the instrument to deliver deadly force, would take us on in a heartbeat. It is troubling, as we feel the loss of someone who died protecting us...and the fear.

Since Professor Samuel G. Chapman's book, *Cops, Killers and Staying Alive: The Murder of Police Officers in America* was published in 1986, much has been done to reduce police fatalities. Fueled by the officer survival movement, which first became a significant force in the 1980s, we've seen improvements in training, equipment, legislation, and administrative support, all aimed at lowering the toll. But the commitment to greater safety in law enforcement must not abate for, in the war on the streets, unlike in military actions, there is no acceptable level of casualties.

For trainers, planners, decision-makers, administrators, supervisors, and even line officers who want to know what more can be done, Professor Chapman's new book, *Murdered on Duty: The Killing of Police Officers in America*, is an excellent resource. In the first four chapters, Professor Chapman updates and expands his meticulous research on the nature of police murders, focusing primarily on a single state's experience, that of Oklahoma from 1950–1994, as reflective of the problem nationally. Going far beyond dry statistics, Chapman offers intriguing facts, reconstructs case histories that disclose the human stories behind the numbers, and presents critiques that reveal the sad truth that careless or complacent officers contribute to their own deaths in at least one of every two fatalities.

Close study of this portion of the book can be a gold mine for imaginative instructors who want to develop dynamic training scenarios that closely simulate real-life attacks on officers. It is also a good wake-up call for street cops, a grim reminder that they are vulnerable more often, and in more situations, than they may like to think.

In the concluding portion of his book, Professor Chapman carefully sets out a broad-based action agenda that could strikingly improve an officer's chances on the street. These range from new areas of emphasis in training (more instruction in verbal persuasion techniques, what he calls "the best police come-along") to what The Brass can do (improving procedures manuals) to needed legislative countermeasures (mandating changes in license plate display). This section can be motivating for police administrators, city managers, citizen groups, researchers, and lawmakers looking to make contributions to the officer survival cause.

Along the way, Professor Chapman vividly reminds readers that the fight for police safety is ever-changing. As improved body armor and better sidearms have lessened some threats, others have arisen: criminals deliberately ram patrol cars to detonate airbags and trap officers inside; drug traffickers create lethal environments by carelessly brewing their wares with toxic chemicals in clandestine laboratories and two-bit hoodlums, emulating behavior seen in the movies and on TV, attack police. In forms that we have yet to see, "Attacks on law enforcement are going to continue," Professor Chapman warns, sensing the worst may be yet to come.

Professor Chapman's is a voice that demands attention and respect. He speaks with authority from many vantage points: he has been in the trenches of police work, as a street cop with the Berkeley, California Police Department, and as police chief of the Multnomah County Sheriff's Department in Portland, Oregon. He has served as assistant director of President Johnson's National Crime Commission, and as director of the exhaustive Police Assaults Study, which established him as a leading authority on violence against law enforcement personnel. As a teacher and researcher, he has filled professorships at Michigan State University and the University of Oklahoma, as well as instructing U.S. military personnel in several foreign countries. Chapman has extensive experience in real-world politics, too, having served eleven years as an elected member of the city council and as vice-mayor of Norman, Oklahoma. And he is a frequent contributor to the professional literature, his numerous publications being regularly cited by scholars and referred to in court proceedings.

His background as an officer, chief, teacher, researcher, politician and writer have assured that *Murdered on Duty* conveys unique information in a readable form. It is a book that deserves study—and application.

"Cop fighting," as Professor Chapman refers to assaults on officers, is a "national disgrace." He writes, "It must be dealt with... The effects of [police] deaths on families, colleagues and police agencies is irreversible, but the losses can be given value... by learning from the experiences and then using that knowledge to prevent further line-of-duty killings...."

Murdered on Duty is a good place to begin understanding and overcoming the challenges we face in law enforcement today.

Charles Remsberg

PREFACE

This book began to take form in 1951, in Berkeley, California, where I patrolled as a street cop, working nights while going to graduate school at the University of California. Like other officers, I had my share of serious scrapes, and on several occasions narrowly missed becoming a casualty. In the 1960s, as police chief of the 250-member Multnomah County Sheriff's Police Department in Portland, Oregon, accounts of attacks on officers crossed my desk, and the urgent need for research and analysis concerning police deaths and risk reduction became apparent. In 1972, while teaching police science at the University of Oklahoma, I assumed yet another role, that of an elected member of the Norman City Council, on which I served for eleven years. While in that role, one of the city's young officers was murdered while apprehending a felon, again underscoring the need for this study.

This book, then, is a synthesis of my personal experiences as a street cop and my concern for officer safety that took shape while I served as a police administrator, university professor, and a local political figure. Its content sets forth ideas about what street cops, trainers, police administrators, city managers, legislators, and researchers can do to reduce assaults on police, even though they are in highly diverse roles.

Like Americans everywhere, I was deeply touched by the April 19, 1995, cataclysmic bombing of the Alfred P. Murrah Federal Office Building in Oklahoma City. In addition to losing close friends, including a former student, many of the police who helped the Oklahoma City Police and Fire Departments, the FBI and the ATF, and other agencies immediately following that evil deed, were friends and former students. These selfless persons were indelibly affected by that event.

There are some things this book *isn't*. It's not another book on street survival, exhorting officers to duck when shots ring out. It isn't a book of quick fixes to the assaults problem, either, for there are no surefire ways to prevent attacks on police. And it is not a book of light reading, as its content implores people in varied sectors to seriously consider public safety issues which range from training, to legislation, to research.

There are some things this book *is*. It's a book dedicated to life and lifesaving. It says, "Let's do more, much more, than merely wringing our hands and burying our dead in the wake of an officer murder! Let's insist that action be taken on many fronts to reduce police casualties." It's a book which calls for breaking the myopic view that casualty reduction is only a matter of street tactics. And it's a book which frankly states that **50 percent of officers murdered are the principal contributors to their demise through carelessness or complacency**. If only officer carelessness and complacency could be obviated, monumental strides will have been taken to help officers help themselves stay alive!

Now a few words about gender. In some instances, I have used the traditional masculine terms in the interest of readability, hoping that no one will be offended by my use of gender-specific terms and pronouns in this book. The fact that I have opted to use the standard "he-him-his-lawman" form, in a few complex paragraphs, by no means implies that I am insensitive to females or that I am denigrating women in any way. On the contrary, I am keenly aware of and impressed by the increasing numbers of women who have opted to join the police and who, like their male counterparts, have become victims of attacks, some of which have resulted in death. In fact, I am keenly aware that in the Murrah Federal Office Building blast, eight females were among the 20 police employees fatally injured.

Several organizations in Oklahoma have been instrumental in bringing this book to fruition. These include the State Department of Corrections; the State Bureau of Investigation; the Office of the State Medical Examiner; the State Health Department; and the State Council on Law Enforcement Education and Training. Help rendered by the Federal Bureau of Investigation is gratefully recognized. Personnel in the public documents and inter-library loan divisions of the University of Nevada, Reno library were critical to this project.

In addition to the organizations, a host of people helped in this research. Among these are the Honorable Alan J. Couch, Associate

District Judge, Cleveland County, Oklahoma, and Professor David R. Morgan, Henry Bellmon Chair of Public Service and Professor of Political Science at the University of Oklahoma. Others include Steven L. Smith, President of KBFW radio in Bellingham, Washington; Dr. Richard Brand of the Truckee Meadows Community College in Reno, Nevada; Agent Robert L. Stewart of the ATF in Reno, Nevada; Chief James Myers, retired, of the Washoe County Sheriff's Office, Reno, Nevada; Phil Stanley, Superintendent of the Washington Corrections Center in Shelton, Washington; Investigator Jack Dolman of the Washington State Department of Corrections in Shelton, Washington; Bradley A. Albro, Deputy U.S. Marshal in Reno, Nevada; Ronald C. Van Raalte of the Law Enforcement Memorial Foundation, Inc., of Roselle, Illinois; Officer Leigha Struffert of the Reno, Nevada Police Department; and Officer Edward J. Castell, retired, of the Berkeley, California Police Department. These persons were constructive critics, editors, troubleshooters, advisors on form and layout, and all-around performers.

There are four persons who deserve special recognition for their timely, never-ending review of the manuscript as it went through draft after draft. Coordinated by Steve Smith, these include: Corporal Claude Wilcott of the Royal Canadian Mounted Police detachment in Coquitlam, British Columbia, Canada; Constable Rick Chaulk of the RCMP detachment in Maple Ridge, British Columbia, Canada; Corporal Jim Beernink of the Swinomish Police Department in La Conner, Washington; and Officer Charlene Hoch of the Auburn, Washington, Police Department.

Special thanks go to two persons. First, for over 20 years, my friend, Pierce R. Brooks, Los Angeles Police Department, retired, encouraged me to put my thoughts into writing and get them published. His book, "...*Officer Down, Code Three.*,"is *the* classic in officer survival, a standard which will be recognized forever. I am grateful to Pierce for so cogently writing about this special area, which begs for greater attention. Second, I am grateful to Charles Remsberg, the nation's leading expert on officer street survival, for writing the Foreword to this book. His participation has special meaning to me.

Finally, my wife, Dr. Carolyn Hughes Chapman, of the University of Nevada, has been a stalwart throughout the preparation of this book. She not only provided important conceptual counsel and editorial assistance, she brought her extensive skills with the computer to bear on the production of this book. Most importantly, she coauthored Chapter 5, bringing the fruits of her significant career in public school administration, supervision, and curriculum development to bear in shaping the chapter's content and direction. In every way, her imagination, love, support, and encouragement was impressive.

In conclusion, while many helped in the book's preparation, I accept full responsibility for its virtues or limitations. My hope is that *Murdered on Duty: The Killing of Police Officers in America* will serve as a wellspring of ideas and a supermarket of concepts, which people and organizations will draw upon, to help make police officers everywhere safer across the United States and Canada.

Samuel G. Chapman

CONTENTS

	Page
Foreword by Charles Remsberg	v
Preface	ix

Part I
THE ASTOUNDING NUMBERS — 3

Chapter
1. THE POLICE ARE PUNCHING BAGS
   - Some Misleading Data - And What Happened — 7
   - The Early Years of Reporting — 12
   - The Accidental Deaths of Officers — 12
   - Summary — 13

Part II
THE INCIDENT, ACTORS AND DISPOSITION — 15

2. THE INCIDENT — 17
   - How Often Does it Happen? — 17
     - The Chase — 19
   - Activity Performed When Murdered — 20
     - Responding to Disturbance Calls — 21
     - Burglaries in Progress — 22
     - Robberies in Progress — 22
     - Attempting Other Arrests — 23
     - Transporting Prisoners — 23
     - Investigating Suspicious Circumstances — 24
     - Ambushes — 25

	Page
Handling Mentally Deranged Persons	27
Traffic Pursuits and Stops	27
Time and Place of the Killings	28
Month, Day and Hour	28
Daylight or Darkness	31
The Geography of the Killings	32
The Murder Weapon	33
Distance Between the Officer and Suspect	35
The Injuries and Death	36
Alone or Assisted - A Raging Controversy	37
3. THE ACTORS: COPS AND KILLERS	41
Police Officer Victims	41
Gender and Race	41
Birthplace	44
Rank	44
Age	44
Marital Status	47
Prior Law Enforcement Experience	47
Military Service	48
Educational Achievement	48
Suspects	48
Gender and Race	49
Birthplace	50
Age	51
Educational Achievement	52
Occupation and Employment	53
Alcohol and Other Drug Use	53

Past Criminal History	54
What Suspects Were Arrested For	55
Urban vs. Nonurban Arrest Patterns	59
About Convictions	59
4. FROM ARREST TO DISPOSITION	**63**
Getting to Trial	64
Plea Bargaining	65
Representation by Counsel	65
Bail	66
Arrest to Arraignment	67
The Preliminary Hearing to Trial	68
Dismissed Charges	68
Length of Trial	69
Post-Conviction Maneuvers	69
Acquittals	70
Time From Arrest to Sentencing	70
Manslaughter Convictions	70
Sentences, Including the Death Penalty	71
Summary	72

Part III
WHAT TO DO ABOUT ATTACKS ON POLICE   73

5. WHAT OFFICERS NEED TO KNOW: IMPROVING POLICE TRAINING	**77**
Evolving Curriculum	78
Knowledge Essential to Officer Survival	79
Survival Skills	86
Survival Attitudes	90

	Page
Effective Training Strategies	94
Enhancing Engagement	97
Simulations	99
High-Tech Simulations	100
Training to Improve the Odds	101
Summary	102

6. GETTING THE HOUSE IN ORDER — 103

	Page
What The Brass Must Do	103
Procedures Manuals	104
Effective Supervision	104
The Officer With Two Jobs	106
Auxiliary Police	107
Physical Fitness Programs	108
Sharpening Field Operations	109
Offering Variety on Patrol	109
Handling and Transporting Prisoners	109
Police Canine Teams and Officer Safety	114
High-Risk Warrant Executions	117
New Dangers From the Drug World	118

7. TECHNOLOGY AND EQUIPMENT IMPROVEMENTS — 121

	Page
Dispatching, Telephones, and Computers	122
Improving Radio Dispatching	122
Combined Communications	124
Electronic Processing Systems	125
Electronic Car Locators	126
Personal Portable Radio Gear	127
911: A National Emergency Phone Number	127
Computerized Information Systems	129

		Page
	Body Protective Equipment	130
	Bullet-Resistant Vests and Jackets	130
	Riot Helmets and Other Body Armor	132
	De-Militarizing Police Officer Appearance	133
	Special Detection Devices	133
8.	TWO SPECIAL ENTERPRISES: JAILING AND UNDERCOVER ROLES	137
	The Jail Can Be A Dangerous Place	137
	Circumstances in Jails and Lockups	138
	Searching for Contraband	142
	Electronic and Systems Applications to Jail Security	144
	Pretrail Diversion Programs	144
	Undercover Law Enforcement and Cults	145
	Misidentity of Officers by Other Officers	147
	Drug Labs and Toxic Chemicals	148
	Countersurveillance	149
	Dealing With Cults and Urban Guerillas	149
	The Importance of Intelligence	151
	O'er Amber Waves of Pot	151
	Vans, Recreational Vehicles and Motor Homes	152
9.	LEGISLATIVE COUNTERMEASURES	155
	Firearms Control Legislation	157
	Capital Punishment	161
	Assuring That There Is an Autopsy	164
	Mandating License Plate Improvements	166
	Nontransparent or Reflective Glass and Window Tinting	168
10.	OTHER THINGS CAN BE DONE	169
	Informing the Public of the Dangers Facing Police	169

		Page
	Dealing With Chemical Dependency	170
	Television and Media Violence	174
	Survivor Benefits	180
11.	A FERTILE ARENA FOR RESEARCH	183
12.	CONCLUSION	191

Bibliography — 193
Index — 195

MURDERED ON DUTY

PART I

THE ASTOUNDING NUMBERS

Sheriff James Sherron is on record as the first lawman to have been killed in what later became the United States. He succumbed to his injuries in 1717, over 280 years ago! Since then, thousands of others have perished on duty, although just how many is not certain. One source, the Law Enforcement Memorial Association of Roselle, Illinois, notes that at least 35,000 had died through 1995. Another source, the National Law Enforcement Officers Memorial Fund, Inc., of McLean, Virginia reports the toll as about 30,000. Irrespective of the source, sums, and discrepancies, the numbers are massive and herald a national tragedy to which little attention has been afforded.

What is known is that during the 50-year span, 1945 through 1994, about 3,367 American police officers have been **murdered** in the line of duty, an average of over 67 deaths each year. Why is the figure so high? How did things get this way? What are the stories behind the tragedies? And most important, what can be done to reduce the carnage?

Chapter 1

THE POLICE ARE PUNCHING BAGS

Nationally, the number of police murdered on duty in the United States has grown notably since 1960 when the Federal Bureau of Investigation first published annual data which highlighted this type of homicide. That number became greater each year, reaching a high of 134 victims in 1973. While fewer lawmen have been murdered each year since then, there have still been significantly more than the 28 who fell in 1960.

For every police officer murdered on duty, there were 565 others who were assaulted, but without a fatal result. In fact, officers suffered no injuries in many of these instances, but the prospect of a fatal injury had presented itself. In short, there is a lot of cop fighting in America, and police can only feel like punching bags. The number of police officers assaulted and the number who were murdered each year since 1960 is shown in Table 1.1.

TABLE 1.1

THE NUMBER OF ASSAULTS ON POLICE OFFICERS
AND POLICE OFFICERS MURDERED BY YEAR
1960 THROUGH 1994

Year	Total Assaults	Rate Per 100 Officers	Assaults with Injury	Rate Per 100 Officers	Number of Police Officers Murdered	Officer Deaths Owing to Accidents
1960	9,621	6.3	NR*	NR	28	20
1961	13,190	8.3	NR	NR	37	34
1962	17,330	10.2	NR	NR	48	30
1963	16,793	11.0	NR	NR	55	33
1964	18,001	9.9	7,738	4.3	57	31
1965	20,523	10.8	6,836	3.6	53	30
1966	23,851	12.2	9,113	4.6	57	42
1967	26,755	13.5	10,770	5.4	76	47
1968	33,604	15.8	14,072	6.6	64	59
1969	35,202	16.9	11,949	5.7	86	39
1970	43,171	18.7	15,165	6.6	100	46
1971	49,787	18.7	17,631	6.6	129	52
1972	31,763	15.1	12,230	5.8	117	41
1973	32,535	15.0	12,880	5.9	134	42
1974	29,511	15.1	11,468	5.9	132	47
1975	44,867	15.4	18,974	6.5	129	56
1976	49,079	16.8	18,737	6.4	111	29
1977	49,156	15.3	17,661	5.5	93	32
1978	56,130	16.1	21,705	6.2	93	52
1979	59,031	17.3	21,764	6.4	106	58
1980	57,847	16.7	21,516	6.2	104	61
1981	57,116	17.2	20,272	6.1	91	66
1982	55,775	17.5	17,116	5.4	92	72
1983	62,324	16.5	20,807	5.5	80	72
1984	60,153	16.2	20,205	5.4	72	75
1985	61,724	15.8	20,817	5.3	78	70
1986	64,259	16.9	21,639	5.7	66	67
1987	63,842	16.8	21,273	5.6	74	74
1988	58,752	15.9	21,015	5.7	78	77
1989	62,172	16.4	21,893	5.8	66	79
1990	71,794	17.4	26,031	6.3	66	67
1991	62,852	15.5	23,650	5.8	71	52
1992	81,252	17.6	29,673	6.4	63	66
1993	66,975	14.7	24,031	5.3	70	59
1994	64,912	13.5	23,194	4.8	76	62

Source: Federal Bureau of Investigation, Crime in the United States and Law Enforcement Officers Killed and Assaulted (Washington, D.C.: U.S. Government Printing Office). Data were extracted from each document for the years set out above.

*NR: Not reported in Crime in the United States until 1964.

The data in Table 1.1 have been extracted from three major FBI publications. The first, *Crime in the United States: Uniform Crime Reports*, sets out the dimensions of crime in our nation. Each year, the publication discusses the incidence of seven Index Offenses, those classes of crime shown by experience to be most completely reported to the police. An eighth Index Offense, arson, was reported in the document starting in 1978.

Each year, from 1960 through 1983, *Crime in the United States* has included tables or a brief account of assaults on police, and their murders, too. Starting in 1972, the FBI supplemented *Crime in the United States* with a companion publication, *Law Enforcement Officers Killed*, which provided comprehensive statistical data on police killings each year, but little analysis. In 1982, the FBI expanded *Law Enforcement Officers Killed* by adding a section about assaults on police, the publication being appropriately retitled. Hence, since 1982, *Crime in the United States* reported only summarily about police officer casualties, leaving the details to be set out in *Law Enforcement Officers Killed and Assaulted*.

Some Misleading Data—And What Happened

One portion of Table 1.1 warrants clarification, because the figures are highly misleading unless one knows what prompted some dramatic swings. Note that in 1971 there were over **five times** the number of officers assaulted as were victimized in 1960. Was it really **five times** more dangerous to be an officer in 1971 than eleven years earlier? No, not at all. The numbers reflect that it took departments a while to get into the swing of reporting assaults on their officers.

Then, all of a sudden, the assaults data for 1972 indicate that it was **safer** to be a police officer, and dramatically so, in contrast to 1971. It was about the same for 1973, and then, in 1974, it got real safe—if you believe the numbers! That didn't last long, for there was a sharp increase in 1975, and the numbers are, generally, up through 1983. And there are more fluctuations through 1994, some being notable, but for no obvious reason.

Surely it wasn't **safer** to be a police officer from 1972-1974 than in 1971, even though the data lead one to so infer. Rather, the numerical plunge during those years, is explained by a failure of many forces to report attacks on officers to the FBI. For example, in 1971, 21 forces across the nation, serving cities of from 100,000 to 750,000 population, failed to report assaults. One year later, for calendar 1972, 69 forces serving equally large cities, provided no assault data at all! A similar reporting gap characterized the FBI numbers for 1973 and 1974, too.

The underreporting for 1972-1974 may be traced to a major revision in the form on which forces were asked by the FBI to report assaults on officers. Specifically, from 1960 through 1971, the form was very easy to fill out. Shown as Structure One, it included but **three** entries. On January 1, 1972, the annual report form was substantially revised, as the FBI sought to assemble far more detailed assault-related information. The new form, shown as Structure Two, had **175** boxes to complete, a task which apparently proved too daunting for many forces and prompted the misleadingly modest numbers of assaults reported for 1972-1974. Police statisticians became more comfortable with the form as time passed, and more representative numbers were reflected starting in 1975. While the numbers of officers **assaulted** each year are believed to be underreported, the FBI's figures on officers **murdered** are regarded as being accurate.

H-76 (Rev. 8-4-67)	Bureau Budget No. 43-R005.9

**NUMBER OF FULL-TIME LAW ENFORCEMENT EMPLOYEES AS OF DECEMBER 31, 1967
NUMBER OF OFFICERS KILLED AND ASSAULTED**

City _____

County _____

State _____

This form is to be used to report all full-time employees on the payroll of your law enforcement agency as of December 31, 1967. Your figures should show all law enforcement officers (sworn personnel) opposite item 1, and full-time civilian employees opposite item 2. The total of items 1 and 2 should be placed opposite item 3.

Items and Instructions

1. Full-time law enforcement officers *(Include Chief, Sheriff, Commissioner, Superintendent)* .... _____
   Include only full-time law enforcement officers on your agency's payroll as of December 31 who work your usual full-time workweek. Do not count special officers, merchant police or others who are not paid with law enforcement funds.

2. Full-time civilian employees *(Do not count school crossing guards)*. . _____
   Include only full-time civilian employees of your department who worked full-time during December (clerks, stenographers, mechanics, etc., who do not have police powers). Count them if they are on leave with pay. If they are not paid from police funds do not count them.

3. Total full-time law enforcement officers and civilian employees . . . . _____
   (Total of items 1 and 2)

OFFICERS KILLED - Number of full-time law enforcement officers belonging to your organization who were killed in line of duty during the year _____

OFFICERS ASSAULTED - Number of full-time law enforcement officers belonging to your organization who were assaulted in line of duty during the year resulting in:

                                        Injury to employee _____

                                        No injury _____

Do Not Write Here			
Recorded _____			
Reviewed _____	Date	Prepared By	Title
Punched _____			
Verified _____			

                                                                  Chief, Sheriff, Commissioner, Superintendent

Please forward this form by January 22 to: **Director, Federal Bureau of Investigation,
Washington, D. C. 20535**

12-108 (Rev. 4-18-72)   Bureau Budget No. 43-R0500

LAW ENFORCEMENT OFFICERS KILLED OR ASSAULTED

It is requested this report be completed and transmitted with monthly crime reports to: Director, Federal Bureau of Investigation, Uniform Crime Reports, Washington, D. C. 20535. This form should be used to report the number of your officers who were assaulted or killed in the line of duty during the month. Additional information concerning officers killed will be requested by a separate questionnaire.

OFFICERS KILLED
Number of your law enforcement officers killed in the line of duty this month.
By felonious act _____
By accident or negligence _____

Officers Assaulted (Do not include officers killed) - See other side for instructions.

Type of Activity	Total Assaults by Weapon A	Type of Weapon				Two-Man Vehicle F	Type of Assignment						Police Assaults Cleared M
		Firearm B	Knife or Other Cutting Instrument C	Other Dangerous Weapon D	Hands, Fists, Feet, etc. E		One-Man Vehicle		Detective or Special Assign.		Other		
							Alone G	Assisted H	Alone I	Assisted J	Alone K	Assisted L	
1. Responding to "Disturbance" calls (family quarrels, man with gun, etc.)													
2. Burglaries in progress or pursuing burglary suspects..........													
3. Robberies in progress or pursuing robbery suspects..........													
4. Attempting other arrests													
5. Civil disorder (riot, mass disobedience).......													
6. Handling, transporting, custody of prisoners...													
7. Investigating suspicious persons or circumstances													
8. Ambush - no warning..													
9. Mentally deranged....													
10. Traffic pursuits and stops..........													
11. All other..........													
12. **TOTAL (1-11)**													
13. Number with personal injury..													
14. Number without personal injury.													
15. Time of assaults .... AM / PM 12:01 2:00 4:00 6:00 8:00 10:00 12:00													

DO NOT WRITE HERE	Initials
Recorded	
Edited	
Punched	
Verified	
Adjusted	

_____   _____   _____   _____
Month and Year   Agency Identifier   Prepared by   Title

_____   _____   _____
Agency   State   Chief, Sheriff, Commissioner, Superintendent

INSTRUCTIONS FOR PREPARING REPORT

When an officer is assaulted in the line of duty, an entry should be made on the appropriate line for type of activity (lines 1-11), under type of weapons used (columns B-E), and under type of assignment (columns F-L). An entry should also be made in either line 13 (injury) or line 14 (no injury). Also count the assault by the time of day on line 15.

When any of these assaults are cleared, an entry should be made under column M for appropriate activity.

At the end of the month, add all lines under columns B through E and enter in column A. The total of columns F through L should equal the total of columns B through E as entered in column A. Also add all columns down and enter in line 12.

Columns B-E:

If more than one type of weapon is used to commit a single assault, the column encountered moving from left to right (B to E) which shows one of the weapons used should be selected for the entry. Do not enter any of the other different types of weapons which were used.

Columns F-L:

Column F (Two-Man Vehicle) and columns G and H (One-Man Vehicle) pertain to uniformed officers; columns I and J (Detective or Special Assignment) to non-uniformed officers; columns K and L (Other) to officers assaulted while in a capacity not represented by columns F-J such as foot patrol, off duty, etc.

Column M:

In column M count the number of "assault on officer" offenses cleared. Do not count the number of persons arrested for such offenses. Include exceptional clearances.

Lines 1-11:

Indicate the type of police activity the officer was engaged in at the time he was assaulted.

Line 12:

Enter the total of lines 1-11.

Line 13:

Enter the number of assaults from line 12 which resulted in personal injury to the officer.

Line 14:

Enter the number of assaults from line 12 in which there was no injury to the officer.

Line 15:

Enter the total number of assaults on police officers occurring within the appropriate two-hour intervals.

The Early Years of Reporting

Actually, the Federal Bureau of Investigation began reporting data about police officer deaths starting in 1945. That year, and every year through 1959, the Bureau reported the number of police murdered on duty **and** those who lost their lives through accidents. During these years there was **no** distinction made between the type of fatality, it was merely a lump sum of deaths reported each year.

For the record, the number of officers reported by the FBI as having perished each year from both accidents and fatal assaults, from 1945 through 1959, is shown in Table 1.2.

TABLE 1.2

THE NUMBER OF OFFICERS WHO PERISHED FROM FATAL ASSAULTS AND ACCIDENTS 1945 THROUGH 1959

Year	Number	Year	Number
1945	59	1953	63
1946	82	1954	61
1947	67	1955	55
1948	64	1956	46
1949	55	1957	45
1950	36	1958	49
1951	64	1959	49
1952	63		

The Accidental Deaths of Officers

The column farthest to the right in Table 1.1 is included merely for the record. It sets out, by year since 1960, the number of police who lost their lives through **accidents**, not **murder**. These include deaths stemming from motor vehicle, motorcycle or aircraft and helicopter crashes, falls, drownings, or being struck while directing traffic or issuing citations. These numbers, like the data pertaining to murder incidents have been derived from annual reports prepared by the FBI.

Summary

The increasing number of attacks on police has prompted concern about the occupational safety of police, not just from among the officers themselves, but from quarters outside law enforcement. In fact, assaults on police lessen the appeal of law enforcement as a career, polarize the public, and jeopardize the American concept of liberty within the framework of law. Clearly, the numbers set out above are astounding, and some means must be found to reduce attacks on police.

PART II

THE INCIDENT, ACTORS, AND DISPOSITION

Cop fighting across America is a national disgrace and must be dealt with. A logical beginning is to assemble information about the incidents which led to the assaults, some of which result in murder. Then we must determine who the victims and suspects are, and we must examine the fate of those who assault police, including the killers. After analyzing these elements, measures may be identified which could reduce the carnage, preventing other officers from becoming casualties.

Frequent reference is made to two sets of data throughout Part 2 of this book. The first set is information derived from an in-depth analysis of 59 incidents from January 1, 1950 through December 31, 1994, in which 61 Oklahoma police officers, all of whom were male, were murdered on duty.

I compiled an incredible amount of information about these incidents. It was derived from a variety of sources, including the forces for which the victims worked, the Oklahoma State Bureau of Investigation, the Oklahoma Department of Corrections, the Office of the State Medical Examiner, the State Historical Society, the FBI, court records and trial transcripts, death certificates, and autopsy reports. Newspaper accounts and obituaries were helpful in filling data gaps, as were interviews with victims' families, prosecutors, defense counsel, veteran lawmen, witnesses, and trial judges. These sources, and others, provided the threads from which the complicated social and technical fabric of each incident was woven. This research was the basis for making a meaningful analysis of all the interlocking elements in each murder.

The second set of data is information derived from three FBI publications: *Crime in the United States, Law Enforcement Officers Killed,* and *Law Enforcement Officers Killed and Assaulted,* which were described in Chapter 1.

Chapter 2

THE INCIDENT

It is a warm evening, shortly before midnight. Gunfire rings out, breaking the peaceful silence of the Oklahoma night. An officer in uniform, assisted by another member of the force, is attempting to make an arrest. One officer is hit, his torso ripped by slugs from a .38 calibre handgun. This was one of the 61 instances in which officers were murdered in Oklahoma between January 1, 1950 and December 31, 1994.

About 1:00 A.M., in a large Oklahoma city, a lone officer stopped a car for what appeared to be a routine traffic citation. The officer stepped from his car and ordered the three occupants out. The driver, rather than producing his driver's license, drew a .25 calibre automatic handgun and shot the officer three times in the chest and abdomen. As the three prepared to make a getaway, the mortally wounded officer was heard to moan. One man went back to the officer, took the lawman's gun from its holster and coldly fired a fourth shot into the back of the policeman's head. The suspects were arrested within two weeks. This is another way in which an officer met death.

How Often Does It Happen?

The data in Table 2.1 show the date of each incident and the interval, by days, from the last officer murder. There was an average of one officer-murder incident every 282 days over the 45 year span. Two dates—September 3, 1949 and April 19, 1995—are significant, as they reflect the dates of murders immediately previous to and after the 45-year research project. There were 24 incidents where the interval between them was greater than the 282-day average. The greatest interval was the 1,181-day span between the July, 1964, murder of an Oklahoma City officer, and the October, 1967, slaying of a Washita County deputy sheriff. Remarkably, this extraordinary fatal-free interval was almost equalled by the 1,177-day span, from September, 1979 to December, 1982.

TABLE 2.1

THE INTERVAL, BY DAYS, FROM THE LAST PREVIOUS
MURDER INCIDENT IN OKLAHOMA
1950 THROUGH 1994

Date	Days From Last Previous Murder	Date	Days From Last Previous Murder
9-3-49	6	5-21-72	342
6-30-50	300	*7-30-72	70
*5-17-51	321	*9-18-72	50
11-13-51	180	5-02-73	226
12-13-51	30	*4-16-74	349
1-03-52	21	7-25-74	100
6-26-53	540	7-25-74	1 hour
6-27-53	1	6-29-75	339
9-05-53	70	*4-04-77	645
*9-14-53	9	6-18-77	75
6-12-54	271	12-10-77	175
7-11-54	29	5-26-78	167
*7-16-54	5	5-26-78	30 minutes
*12-11-54	148	*9-01-78	98
7-04-56	571	*9-19-79	383
5-20-57	320	*12-09-82	1,177
4-28-58	343	1-05-83	27
1-23-59	270	*10-05-83	273
12-22-60	69	10-27-84	388
*4-26-62	490	*2-02-85	98
5-20-62	24	5-08-85	95
6-16-62	27	6-03-85	26
2-03-63	232	*1-07-86	218
10-11-63	250	6-05-88	880
*7-27-64	290	*9-29-90	846
10-21-67	1,181	*4-22-93	936
7-30-68	283	4-19-95	728
8-12-69	378		
6-28-70	320		
7-28-70	30		
11-02-70	97		
2-17-71	107		
*4-02-71	44		
*6-14-71	73		

*Officers murdered in urban settings, 20 in all.

The Incident

An example of the 35 incidents where the interval between officer murders was shorter than the 282-day average, was the instance when there was only 30 minutes between the slayings of two highway patrol troopers and the killing of a highway patrol lieutenant, during a massive manhunt for two prison escapees, during the Memorial Day weekend of 1978 in rural southern Oklahoma. In 1974, two other incidents occurred, in eastern Oklahoma within about one hour of each other.

The two escapees who so coldly murdered the three highway patrol personnel, were killed by police gunfire at the Caddo, Oklahoma site where the lieutenant was fatally hit by a .12 gauge shotgun blast. The lone killer who murdered the two eastern Oklahoma lawmen within an hour in 1974, was taken alive, tried, and convicted of both killings.

Analyzing the anatomy of confrontation is significant to devising remedies. Therefore, it is important to assemble the facts of each incident, to find out exactly what happened.

The Chase

The chase started at once, when the trail is hottest, thanks to an early scent of trouble. When finally confronted, the suspect may shoot it out with police. On the other hand, facing overwhelming numbers of police and the certainty of arrest, a suspect may take his own life. However, most suspects surrendered meekly, hardly resembling the television-inspired image of macho cop-killers.

In the 59 Oklahoma incidents, most chases were of short duration. In fact, of the 81 suspects in the 61 murders, 55 were cornered within 24 hours! Of these, 41 were arrested, 10 were killed by police in shootouts, and four committed suicide. Of the other 26 suspects, 18 were arrested within one week of the slaying, and five within two weeks. Only two suspects were at large for more than two weeks; one was arrested 43 days after the killing, the other in 198 days. If these two prolonged incidents are excluded, the 66 suspects taken alive were apprehended within an average of but 1.5 days.

Wondrously, not since the April 14, 1949, slaying of a Tulsa officer has a cop-killer escaped detection in Oklahoma! The state's perfect clearance rate in these 59 police-killing incidents over the 45-year span, is a tribute to the skill, investigative tenacity, and ability of the state's police officers and of agencies to work cohesively with each other. The national clearance rate for police killings is almost 95 percent since 1960, the year the national clearance rate was first reported by the FBI.

Activity Performed When Murdered

Table 2.2 shows the types of activities in which officers were engaged at the time of their murder. Unfortunately, not all categories have been consistent over the 35-year period that the FBI has presented data. For example, for the first five years, 1960-1964, the FBI lumped the following into one category: (1) persons murdered while transporting prisoners; (2) officers killed while attempting other arrests; and (3) those who were murdered while making apparently routine traffic stops. Starting in 1965, each of these categories was particularized and shown on its own. Likewise, deaths stemming from ambushes and civil disorders were not specifically categorized and shown until 1965.

TABLE 2.2

LAW ENFORCEMENT OFFICERS KILLED
BY TYPE OF ACTIVITY
1950 THROUGH 1994

Type of Activity	Oklahoma 1950-1994		Nationally 1960-1964		Nationally 1965-1994	
	Number	Percent	Number	Percent	Number	Percent
Responding to disturbance calls (family quarrels, man with gun, etc.)	9	14.8	45	20.0	429	16.3
Burglaries in progress or pursuing burglary suspects	3	4.9	28	12.4	148	5.6
Robberies in progress or pursuing robbery suspects	6	9.8	51	22.7	434	16.5
Attempting other arrests (excludes arrests for Burglaries and Robberies)	17	27.9	62	27.6	587	22.4
Civil disorders (mass disobedience, riot, etc.)	—	—	—	—	14	.5
Handling, transporting, custody of prisoners	6	9.8	—	—	117	4.5
Investigating suspicious persons or circumstances	7	11.5	28	12.4	282	10.7
Ambush (entrapment and premeditation)	3	4.9	—	—	123	4.7
Ambush (unprovoked attack)	1	1.6	—	—	106	4.0
Mentally deranged	1	1.6	11	4.9	71	2.7
Traffic pursuits and stops	8	13.2	—	—	315	12.1
TOTALS	61	100.0	225	100.0	2,626	100.0

The FBI chose to particularize two other categories of events. First, in 1973 the Bureau identified the number of officers murdered while intervening in **family quarrels\domestic disturbance calls**. There were 133 officers fatally injured while so engaged from 1973 through 1994. And, beginning in 1983, the FBI listed annually the number of officers murdered while engaged in **drug related matters**. The FBI attributes 63 deaths to this category over the 12 years to 1995.

From 1965-1994, there is a remarkable similarity in seven of the eleven activity categories of the 61 Oklahoma victims with the activities of the 2,626 officers killed nationally. However, there are notable dissimilarities in three categories: (1) burglaries; (2) robberies in progress; and (3) handling prisoners.

One can only speculate as to why Oklahoma lawmen have had such good fortune in handling hot burglary and robbery calls, but such dismal luck in transporting prisoners, in contrast with police nationwide. It certainly isn't because the state lacks burglars or robbers, for Oklahoma's crime rate is hardly modest. At the same time, Oklahoma has a very high ratio of people in penal institutions when compared with figures nationwide, which suggests that there have been high numbers of police-suspect confrontations indicating that inquisitive lawmen may send more cons to the penitentiary.

Responding to Disturbance Calls

Nine of the 61 officers were gunned down while responding to disturbance calls. Many of these deaths occurred as officers intervened in domestic disputes, an activity which is fraught with danger. In seven of these instances, there were two or more officers present, while in two cases the officers were alone. In one of these solo incidents, an officer in a very small town was murdered by a man furious because his son had been arrested. In the second incident, an Ardmore assistant chief responded to a domestic spat involving two men and a woman, and was mistakenly shot as the third party in a love triangle! The chief was gunned down in the driveway as he sought to determine what had prompted an earlier call for help from that home.

One murder, where the victim was assisted, happened during rodeo season in July. It was shortly after midnight when police got a call from a hotel clerk reporting the theft of a shotgun. Three officers and a security guard started up an outside stairway to come in from behind and thereby "surprise" the thief, who was reported to be very drunk and holed up on the second floor. The suspect suddenly leaped onto a second floor landing and fired, killing the officer. The suspect committed suicide before he could be captured.

Burglaries in Progress

Three of 61 Oklahoma officers were murdered while intervening during burglaries in progress. The percentage of officers so murdered is somewhat below the national rate for the 35 year span.

One of the Oklahoma deaths is a virtual rerun of a scene which has plagued police everywhere for decades. About 1:00 A.M. on a Thursday morning in December, a grocery store security officer, alerted by noises, called in police to check the building. Two officers in one patrol unit responded. The two police and the security officer surprised four suspects in the act of burglary. From outside, officers ordered the suspects to surrender and come out of the store. A pistol shot, fired from inside, hit an officer in the chest, killing him instantly. One suspect was killed by return fire. Three other suspects fled and were arrested in Fort Worth, Texas, a few days later. Christmas was bleak in Ardmore, because a well-liked 29-year-old officer was dead. He left a wife and three small youngsters.

Robberies in Progress

The reason far fewer Oklahoma lawmen have lost their lives while intervening during hot robberies than officers nationally, may be partly explained by comparing robbery crime index rates. In 1994, the robbery index crime rate per 100,000 population for the nation as a whole was almost double the 128.1 rate in Oklahoma, a pattern which has been consistent year after year.

One fatality, during a robbery, is particularly interesting as it shows the by-chance nature of some of these incidents. It occurred in a cafe in a very small Oklahoma town when a deputy sheriff had just finished his supper and was walking out the door to his patrol car. He had not noticed the robber, who likewise, had not been aware of the deputy's presence. The two came literally nose-to-nose, startling each other, as the robber was in the process of entering the establishment to hold up the place. The deputy was hit in the chest by one blast at close range from a .20 gauge shotgun. The felon was arrested soon after.

Attempting Other Arrests

A Tulsa detective was assigned to help four federal agents execute a search warrant in a narcotics case. Upon reaching the house, the five officers split up. The city detective and one agent covered the back while the other three agents knocked on the front door and charged inside. The agents who entered ducked just in time as a man pulled a .25 calibre pistol, and fired. Then, the suspect yanked the back door open and leaped outside. His second shot missed another agent but a third shot hit the Tulsa detective in the heart. The suspect was arrested at once, charged, and convicted of murder.

This tragic incident happened to one of the 17 officers murdered while attempting to make an arrest for a crime other than a robbery or a burglary in progress. In 13 of the 17 incidents, the victims were in the presence of at least one other officer and in some cases, many others. The common denominator in each of these incidents was the fact that the department had advance notice that a wanted suspect was at a particular location. Understandably, several police were dispatched to the scene. Yet, several of the killings resulted when an officer unexpectedly confronted a hot suspect.

Transporting Prisoners

Six officers were murdered while transporting prisoners. In four of the incidents, the suspects were **not** handcuffed, which proved to be the prime contributing factor to the murders. In one of the incidents, the person to be transported had neither been handcuffed nor searched, yet the arrest centered around a felony. In another incident, an officer in a large metropolitan area went to a hotel to pick up and transport a rape suspect who was already in the custody of other personnel. Carelessly, the suspect was neither searched nor handcuffed before the transporting officer put him into the back of the police car. On the way to jail the unrestrained suspect suddenly grabbed the officer's clipboard and crashed it down on the lawman's head. The car jumped a curb as the officer tried to fight off the suspect. The man drew a 7.65 Beretta pistol which had been concealed on his person but had not been detected because no search had been made. Shot in the heart, death was instantaneous. The suspect was apprehended within minutes.

In yet another instance, two officers were transporting two felony suspects to the county jail. The prisoners were handcuffed with their hands in front, for their comfort, and they sat placidly in the back seat. Suddenly, one reached over the front seat and grabbed the steering wheel, jerking it abruptly, which caused the cruiser to crash into the oncoming traffic. The officers were killed instantly; the two prisoners were not seriously injured.

In addition to carelessness, the high incidence of murder while transporting prisoners in Oklahoma may be linked to the state's geography. There are hundreds of rural communities, many of which have no jail, or one which is old, substandard, and not safe. Also, commute distances between facilities are great, which maximizes officer exposure to attack when transporting prisoners to state hospitals or to the state penitentiary. Officers may become inattentive and bored when they make these kinds of runs regularly, forgetting about the grave dangers involved. In several of these deaths, officers would not have been victimized had they heeded standard police procedures.

The failure to adequately search prisoners before transport, the failure to handcuff prisoners during transport, the absence of a device separating front from rear cabs, the repetitious nature of transport missions, and perhaps even boredom and fatigue inherent in transporting prisoners, are all culprits in the murders. Furthermore, the failure to handcuff prisoners' hands **behind** their backs or to use belly chains can lead to attacks on police.

Investigating Suspicious Circumstances

It is hard to pinpoint why a greater percentage of Oklahoma lawmen were murdered than those nationally, while investigating suspicious persons or circumstances. While officers are very inquisitive by training, there is no reason to believe that Oklahoma's lawmen are any more so than officers across the United States.

One of the seven Oklahoma murders is representative of what could happen anywhere, day or night, when officers check out their suspicions. Early one morning an officer observed a car parked at a service station after hours. He knew that the car had not been there an hour earlier which prompted the investigation. As he warily approached the car an unseen occupant unloaded a shotgun into the officer. The assailant was arrested, convicted and sentenced to life in prison.

Another Oklahoma officer died as he stood in the parking lot of a tavern doing follow-up work on a theft reported the day before. Suddenly, the father of one of the men being questioned stepped up to the officer and started shooting. The officer died instantly, having had no chance to defend himself. His murderer was sentenced to life in prison.

Ambushes

Nationally, the ambush attack did not play a significant role in the killings of police prior to 1970. The FBI reported that from 1960-69, 43 officers were murdered by attacks from ambush, an average of 4.3 deaths per year. However, from 1970 to 1979, with two exceptions, the toll year-by-year rose at a disconcerting rate. From 1980 through 1994 the number seemed to have stabilized, except in 1991, which was still below the peak years' totals. The sums from 1970 through 1994 are shown in Table 2.3.

TABLE 2.3

OFFICER DEATHS FROM AMBUSH ATTACKS
1970 THROUGH 1994

Year	Number	Year	Number
1970	19	1983	9
1971	20	1984	8
1972	14	1985	7
1973	0	1986	5
1974	9	1987	4
1975	10	1988	7
1976	13	1989	5
1977	4	1990	9
1978	12	1991	11
1979	11	1992	7
1980	7	1993	4
1981	9	1994	6
1982	9		

The dramatic national upsurge for 1970-72 may be linked to the hot-button sociopolitical environment in which police found themselves during the turbulent days of campus unrest, anti Vietnam War demonstrations, and street violence.

The Oklahoma picture is the reverse of that nationally. In fact, all four ambush murders of unwary Sooner lawmen occurred relatively early, one death each in 1951, 1954, 1958 and 1962. All were in nonurban places and had nothing to do with war or national political issues. Investigation revealed just the opposite; these were angry persons settling grudges against the victims, the officers having had no sense of how deeply the assailants felt.

Three of the four Oklahoma ambush victims were alone. The one victim, who was in the presence of another person was, for all intents and purposes, alone, as he was accompanied by a nonpolice trained part-time city employee who was also murdered. Two of the incidents occurred at night, and two during daylight which suggests that darkness was not a major ingredient of ambush attacks.

Handling Mentally Deranged Persons

Instances where officers must deal with persons suffering from apparent mental aberrations are among the most unpredictable and emotional confrontations that police face. One Oklahoma case is illustrative. At 10:30 A.M. one Tuesday in July, a distraught man reported to police that his 74-year-old father had barricaded himself in his house, was armed, and wouldn't come out. The son asked police to help persuade the elderly man to seek medical attention. Three lawmen drove to the call in two vehicles, the officer well acquainted with the elderly person was alone in his car.

The two other officers, unfamiliar with the man, parked well away from the house to await the son's arrival. To their dismay, the lone officer pulled his car up next to the house. As the two officers saw the elderly man prepare to fire, they shouted a warning, but it was too late. As the officer scrambled back to his car, there was a deadly shot to the forehead from a .20 gauge shotgun. The confused elderly man was later killed by police gunfire.

Traffic Pursuits and Stops

That there were no murders stemming from traffic stops or pursuits in Oklahoma for over 20 years, from 1950 to mid-1970, is nothing short of miraculous, considering that thousands of traffic stops were made each month across the state. But from mid-1970 through 1994, eight officers were murdered while engaged in such activity. Interestingly, it was a routine traffic stop made by an Oklahoma Highway Patrol trooper on April 19, 1995, when he saw a car without a license plate which unwittingly lead to the arrest of Timothy McVeigh, the prime suspect in the evil bombing, just hours earlier, of the Murrah Federal Office Building in Oklahoma City which took 168 lives.

Many traffic stops take place in isolated settings by personnel working alone at night. Moreover, almost all are treated as routine by officers, unless their senses are piqued to something unusual. So, while an officer may perceive a traffic stop as "routine," it may indeed be viewed differently by the driver owing to some earlier criminal activity about which an officer is unaware. In such circumstances, the officer is a sitting duck. This is what happened to a highway patrol trooper who was viciously gunned down about 11:45P.M. near Ardmore in an isolated setting. The trooper didn't know that the speeding driver he had stopped had been involved only hours earlier in a murder and a kidnapping. To the trooper the stop was routine, to the driver it was a defining moment of truth.

Time and Place of the Killings

When and where officers were murdered is important information. So are factors such as the day, month, season, and daylight or darkness. Urban and rural characteristics of the cases should be identified, too, as should the frequency pattern. These factors are described next.

Month, Day and Hour

Incidents that occur just before midnight in May, June, or July are the times when lawmen in Oklahoma are most likely to be murdered. In fact, 28 of the 59 incidents took place during these warm weather months. Fifteen of the 20 incidents that occurred in urban areas took place from April through September, usually the warmest periods with the liveliest night life.

Neither the Oklahoma nor the national tabulations showing the month of the incident are useful in predicting when the next police officer may be murdered. However, at least as pertains to Oklahoma, the figures disclose that in warmer months officers face the greatest danger. This contrasts sharply with the national picture, as data in Table 2.4 show.

TABLE 2.4

OKLAHOMA AND NATIONAL INCIDENTS BY MONTH OF THE YEAR 1950 THROUGH 1994

Month of the Year	1950-1994 Oklahoma Data		1968-1994* National Data	
	Number	Percent	Number	Percent
January	4	6.8	242	10.0
February	3	5.1	208	8.6
March	—	—	178	7.4
April	6	10.2	210	8.7
May	8	13.5	197	8.2
June	11	18.6	192	8.0
July	9	15.2	185	7.7
August	1	1.7	199	8.3
September	6	10.2	191	7.9
October	4	6.8	185	7.7
November	2	3.4	198	8.2
December	5	8.5	225	9.3
TOTALS	59	100.0	2,410	100.0

*The FBI national data for deaths by month are not shown prior to 1968.

The most dangerous day of the week is remarkably congruent in both the Oklahoma and national data. Table 2.5 shows that danger lurks at times other than on weekends, although many people believe that weekends hold more potential for crime. This may be so, but apparently not to the degree popularly imagined.

TABLE 2.5

OKLAHOMA AND NATIONAL INCIDENTS BY DAY OF THE WEEK 1950 THROUGH 1994

Day of the Week	1950-1994 Oklahoma Data		1960-1994 National Data	
	Number	Percent	Number	Percent
Sunday	8	13.5	354	12.4
Monday	9	15.3	395	13.9
Tuesday	6	10.2	386	13.5
Wednesday	7	11.8	389	13.7
Thursday	9	15.3	436	15.3
Friday	9	15.3	460	16.2
Saturday	11	18.6	426	15.0
TOTALS	59	100.0	2,846	100.0

The time when incidents occur is shown in Table 2.6. The Oklahoma data differ from the national figures in that while almost five of every ten police murder incidents nationally happened between 6:00P.M. and 2:00A.M., about two of every three incidents in the Sooner state occurred during this span. However, the most lethal two-hour period by far in both data sets is from 10:00P.M. to midnight.

TABLE 2.6

OKLAHOMA AND NATIONAL INCIDENTS BY HOUR OF THE DAY 1950 THROUGH 1994

Hour of the Day	1950-1994 Oklahoma Data		1960-1994 National Data	
	Number	Percent	Number	Percent
12PM-2AM	8	13.5	379	13.4
2AM-4AM	3	5.1	296	10.5
4AM-6AM	2	3.4	130	4.6
6AM-8AM	1	1.7	75	2.6
8AM-10AM	3	5.1	146	5.2
10AM-NOON	7	11.9	182	6.4
NOON-2PM	—	—	191	6.7
2PM-4PM	2	3.4	193	6.8
4PM-6PM	3	5.1	241	8.5
6PM-8PM	6	10.2	251	8.9
8PM-10PM	10	16.9	345	12.2
10PM-12PM	14	23.7	403	14.2
TOTALS	59	100.0	2,832	100.0

Daylight or Darkness

Darkness, a phantom time, is another factor which adds to the risk of being attacked. Darkness is seen as cover by the suspect prone to violence. Night may also encourage attacks on police because suspects believe that darkness will aid their escape and reduce the chance that their deed will be soon discovered. The evening hours are the drinking hours, too, and the time when aimless people look for excitement and confrontation. The Oklahoma data give a revealing picture of how daytime-nighttime conditions affect police murders. Just over two of every three of the 59 incidents occurred under darkness, while three more were at dusk, in the shadows of the day.

Nighttime proved the most dangerous time for officers to attempt to make arrests, respond to disturbance calls, and investigate suspicious persons or circumstances. Almost all of the burglaries and robberies-in-progress murders occurred at night, as did most slayings at traffic stops. By contrast, five of the six transportation murders occurred in daylight.

The Geography of the Killings

Pinpointing just where the killings occurred within the state is important to isolating the urban-rural distinctions in the incidents. This may help explain some of the social variables of police officer murders and contribute to devising effective countermeasures. Almost 68 percent of Oklahoma's population resides in one of the four urbanized regions classified in 1990 as Metropolitan Statistical Areas (MSAs) by the United States Bureau of the Census. These MSAs included 1,869,842 of the state's 3,145,585 population in 1990. The MSAs are those regions around and including Oklahoma City (958,839 people); Tulsa (708,954 people); Lawton (111,486 people); and Enid (56,735 people). The 33,828 residents of Sequoyah County, in far eastern Oklahoma, are classified as part of the Fort Smith, Arkansas, MSA.

While the state's population is definitely urban, and becoming more so all the time, the geography of Oklahoma's 59 murder incidents is decidedly nonurban. For example, 39 of the 59, or almost 2 of every 3 incidents, occurred outside the state's MSAs.

The urban-rural distinction reveals a very significant finding which should not be overlooked by police: **there is as much danger in rural places as in the cities!** Hence, no officer should feel secure from attack merely because of a feeling of being among friends in the country or in a small city. Guns abound in rural as well as in urban Oklahoma and, clearly, this hardware is used for more than sport and varmint control!

The 20 urban incidents included the murder of four Tulsa officers, eight with the Oklahoma City force, and one each from Norman, Catoosa, Spencer, and Oklahoma City's Will Rogers World Airport. In addition, two Oklahoma Highway Patrol troopers were murdered while serving in the Oklahoma City MSA, and two while serving in the Tulsa MSA. No sheriff's personnel were victims in urban areas.

On the other hand, of the 39 nonurban incidents in which officers were murdered, 18 were in small city forces, 14 from sheriff's departments, six were highway patrol personnel, and there was a state narcotics agent murdered in a small city.

The Murder Weapon

As every officer knows, police, all too often, must resolve incidents where firearms are involved. It is touchy work, highly volatile, and calls for extraordinary officer presence, judgement, and quick thinking. Table 2.7 shows that there is an incredible amount of firepower being unleashed on police officers. What's more, if a bullet finds its mark, it is very likely to be fatal. The late J. Edgar Hoover underscored this fact in the September, 1967, issue of the *FBI Law Enforcement Bulletin*: "The readily available lethal firearm, seven times more deadly than other murder weapons, is a major factor [in officer killings]."

TABLE 2.7

THE NUMBER AND PERCENTAGES OF OFFICERS
MURDERED IN OKLAHOMA AND NATIONALLY
BY TYPE OF WEAPON
1950 THROUGH 1994

Type of Weapons	1950-1994 Oklahoma		1960-1994 Nationally	
	Number	Percent	Number	Percent
Handguns	40	65.6	2,021	71.0
Shotguns	16	26.2	286	10.0
Rifles	3	4.9	360	12.6
Knife, other cutting instrument	—	—	45	1.6
Bomb	—	—	10	.4
Personal Weapons: hands, fists, feet	—	—	20	.7
Other: clubs, autos, etc.	2	3.3	104	3.7
TOTALS	61	100.0	2,846	100.0

The handgun, by far the most destructive, commonly available lethal weapon police face, was used in 40 of the fatal assaults on Oklahoma lawmen. Long guns, 16 shotguns and three rifles, were used in 19 of the murders. An automobile was used to snuff out the lives of two lawmen. Oklahoma's rural setting, with so much land in cattle ranches and with thousands of large farms where wheat and soybeans are grown and oil is pumped from the ground, may account for the high incidence of shotguns used to kill police in contrast to rifles. Many, many ruralites own shotguns for killing varmints and bird hunting, so a shotgun in a pickup truck gun rack is not an uncommon sight in the Sooner State.

The handguns are a varied array in the staggering arsenal available to the Oklahoma criminal, as shown in Table 2.8.

TABLE 2.8

THE NATURE OF HANDGUNS USED IN THE MURDER OF OKLAHOMA POLICE 1950 THROUGH 1994

Weapon*	Times Used
.38 calibre	12
.25 calibre automatic	7
.32 calibre automatic	5
.22 calibre automatic	4
.325 magnum	1
.357 magnum	6
.44 magnum	1
.380 calibre automatic	2
.45 calibre	1
7.65 Beretta pistol	1
.38 or .357	1

*One officer was shot with two different handguns.

Nationally, as in Oklahoma, the handgun is by far the most dangerous weapon police must face. Such weapons, highly concealable, are much more likely to be pulled on officers than either unwieldy shotguns or rifles.

Unfortunately, the very weapon a lawman carries for his own protection sometimes is turned against him. For example, nationally over the 28 years 1967-94, handguns were used in 1,767 murders of lawmen. In 314 (or 17.8 percent) of these incidents officers lost control of their weapons and were murdered with them. In essence, the victim officer had unwittingly armed an unarmed suspect. During 45 years in Oklahoma, six officers were murdered with their own guns, while two others were killed by guns taken from their partners. These data underscore the fact that officers must wage a titanic struggle before allowing themselves to be disarmed! Firearms retention, indeed, is directly related to officer survival.

Distance Between the Officer and Suspect

The shooting erupted suddenly and came at close range in most of the Oklahoma incidents. With no warning, the victim was confronted by a firearm. There was one or more shots, and he was hit. Only a few officers had time to draw their weapons and fire. Death came with practically no warning, and some probably never suspected what was taking place until the first bullet ripped through their body. These characteristics underscore the urgent need for better, more timely safeguards for officers since, in most cases, police are victimized when they least expect to be.

Table 2.9 shows that cop killing comes at close quarters. In fact, over 50 percent of victim officers are within an arm's reach of death when hit by bullets. And, almost three of every four gunshot hits come from within ten feet! This confirms the fact that the action is often sudden, without warning, and deadly. There is no room for officer error, and there is little chance for reaction after the first shot. These data, and those in Table 2.7, confirm that it is handguns, not rifles, shotguns, knives, or clubs that usually kill officers.

TABLE 2.9

LAW ENFORCEMENT OFFICERS MURDERED IN OKLAHOMA AND NATIONALLY SHOWING THE DISTANCE BETWEEN THE VICTIM OFFICER AND THE MURDERER 1950 THROUGH 1994

Distance in Feet	Oklahoma 1950-1994		Nationally 1972-1994	
	Number	Percent	Number	Percent
0-5	33	54.1	1,028	53.6
6-10	11	18.0	390	20.3
11-20	12	19.7	258	13.5
21-50	2	3.3	132	6.9
Over 50	3	4.9	109	5.7
TOTALS	61	100.0	1,917	100.0

The Injuries and Death

In all, the 61 Oklahoma victims took an average of almost two hits each, as a total of 103 shots found their marks. Even this figure may be a few hits low, owing to one case where the postmortem account was vague, reporting "several hits." Oklahoma officers were struck by 32 shots in the head/neck region; 58 times in the torso/body; and the victims' hands, arms and legs suffered five wounds. There were eight shots, which hit the victims, but where they entered was not specified in postmortem accounts.

Close range, the element of surprise, and a hit in at least one vital area were reasons for instantaneous death. Forty-nine of the murdered Oklahoma officers died either instantaneously or within one hour of the shooting. Ten others died within six hours. One lived 36 hours, while another officer survived six days before succumbing to his wounds.

An officer, gravely wounded but able to shoot his assailant, is a frequent television phenomenon. But does it often occur in the real world? Sometimes, but only one officer in Oklahoma was able to kill his assailant. A few other victims were able to return fire, inflicting nonfatal wounds, while some fired but found no mark. Most victims never got off a shot.

Alone or Assisted—A Raging Controversy

Thirty of the 61 Oklahoma officers were working alone and were unassisted at the time they were murdered. Of the 31 victims who were in the company of other police personnel, eleven were working in one-officer cars; 15 were part of a two-officer patrol team; and four of the victims were detectives. The last of the 31 victims was a lieutenant who was in a squad car with another officer when he was shot.

There were 36 victims murdered under cover of darkness. Of these, 17 were unassisted. There were 22 deaths during daylight hours. In eleven of these, the victims were unassisted. Of the three deaths at dusk, two officers were unassisted when killed.

Of the 20 victims working in urban places when murdered, five were alone working at night, and five were alone when murdered during the day. Six officers working with partners were slain at night. Four other lawmen in one-officer cars were murdered, but these victims were being backed up when killed.

Of the 39 officers murdered in nonurban settings, six were unassisted and murdered during daylight, while 14 were alone and murdered during darkness. There were two rural officers who were patrolling alone when slain at dusk. Ten rural officers were assisted when murdered at night; seven were daylight victims who fell while in the company of other lawmen.

Dry as these numbers may be, they tell the story of lives lost in the line of duty, officers upholding the laws they pledged to enforce. So it is timely to question the assignment of officers one to a patrol car to see if that practice contributes to the murder of police officers.

What is striking about the deaths of the 30 lone victims, as well the 31 others who were in the presence of other officers, is that many of the murders were preventable. It appears that a lack of training, a moment of carelessness, over-reliance on other officers, a guess which proved wrong about how other officers were going to behave, and an underestimation of apparent circumstances, contributed to several deaths. The failure to comply with some standard communication or field tactical procedure was central to the deaths of several officers. These lapses characterized not just a few men working singly, but were apparent in cases where several personnel were present. The issue, then, is NOT purely one-vs-two officer motor patrols. It is far broader, and must include a candid evaluation of officer carelessness as a factor which contributed to murder.

Owing to the nominal data base involved in the research, no absolute conclusion can be drawn about one-vs-two officer motor patrol assignments and the relative safety inherent in solo or dual staffing. But the fact that more assisted officers were murdered during the night than officers working alone suggests that two personnel in the car are not necessarily any safer. At the same time, it cannot be persuasively argued that it is more dangerous to serve in a two-officer motor patrol team than in a solo unit either, though these teams get into their share of scrapes.

There are, of course, disadvantages to patrolling alone. But with today's instantaneous communications and other electronic systems, assistance is no more than a radio call away. So the alone-vs-assisted motor patrol controversy swirls, and this research fails to provide a clear-cut answer as to the relative safety of these sharply different patrol staffing patterns.

The only fact about one- and two-officer motor patrols proved by the Oklahoma study is the near certainty that the issue will surface with intensity and emotion every time an officer working alone is murdered. The issue can become politicized, too. For example, soon after a highway patrol trooper was murdered north of rural Altus, Oklahoma's governor announced that the probe of the shooting would include studying the patrol's policy of having troopers cruise alone. In the wake of another trooper's murder, an Ardmore legislator co-authored a bill making two-officer motor patrolling mandatory at night in cities over 10,000 population, a measure which failed to become law. The death of yet another trooper prompted the chief of the Oklahoma Highway Patrol to state that the incident emphasized the need for two troopers in the cars at all times. At once, the governor announced a plan to put troopers out in pairs, but nothing of any substance happened in the wake of the apparent political hoopla, for after a few weeks of being paired up, troopers returned to solo patrols, by their near unanimous choice!

These three incidents are symbolic of this continuing controversy. On one side is the notion that there is safety in numbers. Advocates of one-officer motor patrols, on the other hand, assert that proper training, constant vigilance, and ever-present radio communications provide the unassisted officer a safety net with all the advantages of two-officer patrol, while concurrently intensifying area coverage and maximizing officer visibility.

The issue remains an open one, highly contentious, and certain to surface again, again and again—especially in the wake of a murder where the officer was serving alone.

Chapter 3

THE ACTORS: COPS AND KILLERS

Each force wonders if one of its officers will be the next to suffer a fatal injury. While hoping not, it is inevitable that murders will occur and other lawmen will die, as 61 did in Oklahoma between 1950 and 1994.

After finding out the circumstances, one wonders about the characteristics of the victims and suspects. Are there any common denominators? Were the players acquainted before the event? Is there a racial angle? Pre-incident antagonism? In short, what happened?

Police Officer Victims

He is a 40-year-old Oklahoma native, white, in uniform serving as a trooper, sheriff's deputy, or city police officer. If he is not an Oklahoma Highway Patrol trooper or an Oklahoma City officer, he works for a small nonurban force, is married, has two youngsters and has been a police officer for about seven years. He has served in the armed forces, is a high school graduate, and had some college hours, but no degree. He was on motor patrol. Other officers were on duty, but did not witness his murder. He was cut down by sudden gunfire and died within one hour of the incident. This profile sets out the "typical" victim, although, understandably, no two victims or incidents are the same.

Gender and Race

All 61 Oklahoma victim officers were male. Of these, 56 were white, one was an American Indian, and four were black. The four black officers were murdered by black assailants, while the Indian officer, a sheriff, was murdered by an American Indian. Of the 56 white officers, 41 were murdered by whites, 13 by blacks, and two by American Indians.

Women, who only since about 1975 have attained equal footing with males in police departments across the United States, comprise about nine percent of the law enforcement work force. While a nominal presence, police departments continue to actively induct, train, and assign greater numbers of female police officers to street patrol duty, so their number is increasing, as is their vulnerability to victimization.

Until the April 19, 1995 federal office building blast in Oklahoma City, there had never been a female police officer murdered on duty in Oklahoma, though many females have been victims of nonfatal assaults and one had been fatally injured in a car accident. But not many forces nationwide have had a female officer murdered.

The very nature of the job, *not gender*, is the issue when women officers are slain. The first female officer murdered on duty was Anna Hart, a 45-year-old deputy sheriff of the Hamilton County, Ohio, sheriff's police. Deputy Hart was working in the jail the evening of July 24, 1916 when she was beaten to death by a prisoner wielding an iron bar.

The second female officer victim was Mary T. Davis, who was in charge of the care and custody of female prisoners in the Wilmington, Delaware, city jail on May 11, 1924. Ms. Davis, without calling for assistance, entered the cell of a female prisoner to see why water was pouring from it and was brutally attacked and left to die as the cell's occupant escaped.

Too soon, the one-hundredth female victim's name will be inscribed on the wall of the National Law Enforcement Officers Memorial in the District of Columbia. As of September, 1996, staff of the Law Enforcement Memorial Foundation, Inc., reported that 86 female police personnel had been fatally injured since the death of deputy Hart. Of these, 38 or 44 percent, succumbed to accidents of which most were traffic-related.

Female police who have been murdered on duty succumbed in events which are similar to those which took the lives of their male counterparts. Houston's first female officer was accidentally shot and killed while in plainclothes on an undercover drug investigation. Something went sour when the victim and a male counterpart were making a drug buy and gunshots erupted. She was shot by a uniformed Houston officer who observed the transaction and felt he had been placed in a life threatening situation. Seven months earlier, a Montgomery, Alabama, female officer, also in a plainclothes undercover assignment, was shot to death while she and her partner attempted an arrest. In fact, many incidents where female officers have been murdered were in these sorts of activities, where the misidentification of police was central to the death.

One of New York City's female officers murdered on duty was a 25 year-old Transit Authority officer with three years of service. She was slain on September 21, 1984, shot twice in the head with her own revolver. Her body was found in a weed-choked vacant lot in the Bushwick section of Brooklyn three hours after she and her male partner had split up to chase a suspected gold-chain snatcher. A 19-year-old male suspect was indicted six days later.

The first female federal officer murdered while on duty was a U.S. Secret Service agent who, with a partner, was conducting surveillance during a Los Angeles investigation. On the evening of June 4, 1980, the two agents in plainclothes were victims of an apparent robbery attempt. Forced from the surveillance vehicle, the victim agent was disarmed and murdered with the .12 gauge shotgun which had been taken from her. The first female FBI agent to die in the line of duty since women became agents in 1972 was murdered in Phoenix, Arizona, on October 5, 1985, while helping other agents arrest an armed robbery suspect.

Forces other than just the big ones, like the District of Columbia, Houston, San Diego, Denver, and New York City have suffered female officer fatalities. Among these are female officers serving Baton Rouge, Louisiana; Aurora, Colorado; Overland Park, Kansas; Huntsville, Texas; Plainfield, New Jersey; Montgomery, Alabama; and the Florida Game and Freshwater Fish Commission.

As more and more females are joining police forces as officers, some are being promoted. Portland, Oregon, was the first major American city to name a female as police chief in March, 1985, when a well qualified woman was selected from among several candidates. Since then, several other very large forces as well as many smaller ones, have been headed by women.

Birthplace

Data assembled principally from obituaries and death certificates revealed the birthplace of each of the 61 Oklahoma officer victims. Thirty-eight were born in Oklahoma and apparently chose to work near the place of their birth, rejecting the pattern of out-migration which characterized many Oklahomans beginning in the 1920s, and which John Steinbeck vividly described in his classic novel, *The Grapes of Wrath*. That many of these 38 native-born Oklahomans were United States military veterans and served on posts across the nation as well as worldwide, but after service chose to return to settings where they felt comfortable, safe, and at ease, underscores how really "local" these slain officers were.

The data also reveal that it was not uncommon for the victims to be murdered at a site relatively near where they were born. In fact, 31 of the 61 officers were murdered within 100 miles of their birthplace and of these, 15 were victimized within 25 miles! Only eight of the 61 were murdered at a locale farther away than 500 miles from their place of birth.

Rank

Although 49 Oklahoma police officers, troopers, city marshals, park rangers, and deputy sheriffs were killed, being promoted did not assure safety. Among executives, five chiefs of police or sheriffs were killed as was one assistant chief, one undersheriff, and one lieutenant. Four detective or uniformed sergeants fell to gunfire, too. The message is that police are murdered, irrespective of rank or role.

Age

Not just young, inexperienced officers were killed in Oklahoma. The average age of the 61 at time of their death was 40 years, 3 months. Checking extremes, one officer was murdered just four days before his 23rd birthday, while three others were but 24 years old. On the other hand, one sheriff's deputy was 69 when murdered while intervening in a stickup in progress. The victims, by age range, are set out in Table 3.1.

TABLE 3.1

OKLAHOMA OFFICERS KILLED, BY AGE RANGE

Age Range	Number of Officers	Percentage
21-25	6	9.8
26-30	13	21.4
31-35	6	9.8
36-40	8	13.1
41-45	6	9.8
46-50	7	11.5
51-55	8	13.1
56-60	4	6.6
61-65	1	1.6
66-	2	3.3
TOTAL	61	100.0

The number of officers murdered by five-year blocks over the past 45 years and their average age is shown in Table 3.2.

TABLE 3.2

NUMBER OF OKLAHOMA OFFICERS MURDERED BY FIVE-YEAR PERIODS 1950 THROUGH 1994

Years	Number of Officers Murdered	Average Age
1950-54	13	46.1
1955-59	4	46.0
1960-64	7	38.4
1965-69	4	41.0
1970-74	13	38.5
1975-79	9	44.8
1980-84	4	27.0
1985-89	5	35.6
1990-94	2	25.5
45 Years	61	40.3

The data in Table 3.2 show two five-year blocks when 13 officers were murdered and a third, 1975-79, which approached the years of greatest lethality. However, there is no consistent pattern. Neither is there a consistent pattern to the age of the victims, although the officers murdered from 1980-84 averaged 19 years less in age than the victims of the 1950s. The officers who perished from 1990-94 were younger than those in any other five-year block.

The 20 officers who were serving in urban settings when murdered averaged 34.7 years of age. Their 41 nonurban counterparts averaged 42.3 years of age. The fact that the nonurban officers are much older than their urban counterparts may be a reflection of less stringent police service entry requirements and less attractive conditions of service and pay in the nonurban forces, especially during the first 25 years of the 45-year study.

The average age of the 12 murdered highway patrol troopers was 36.9, while sheriff's personnel averaged 46.3 years of age when killed. Municipal police victims averaged about 38 years of age.

Marital Status

Nearly all of the 61 Oklahoma victim police officers were married at the time they were fatally wounded. Only two were divorced, and three had never been wed. While the death of these 61 lawmen left 125 children fatherless, several of the surviving children were adults with their own families. One of the officers had been married but a few months, while a veteran highway patrol trooper had been married 43 years. A county sheriff left seven children when he was murdered.

There is a popular notion, seemingly based on mortality figures of American military personnel killed in World War II, the Korean War, and the Vietnamese conflict, that single men will take greater risks with their lives than will married men. Or, as sometimes stated, a married man will be more cautious than a single man who has no home, wife, and family to consider. By no means are these notions supported by the Oklahoma experience.

Whether being married had anything to do with an officer's degree of caution, or reluctance to take chances as circumstances unfolded, is speculative. The data in this study neither confirm nor reject this premise, but they do underscore that an officer of any age may be called upon to face a dangerous situation at any time. This is especially so in rural locales, where each officer wears many hats, and it is not unusual that he or she is the only officer on duty in the jurisdiction, especially at night.

Prior Law Enforcement Experience

The number of years that lawmen had been in police work was determined for 51 of the 61 Oklahoma officers. While their average length of service was 6.9 years, 27 of them had less than five years with their parent force.

The fact that an officer has been in police work for years does not exempt him or her from becoming a victim. For example, several seasoned personnel fell prey: two highway patrol troopers had, respectively, 32 and 25 years service when they were murdered by two vicious prison escapees in 1978. A police chief was just finishing his 22nd year in law enforcement when he lost his life responding to a disturbance call. Another officer was on the job only two weeks, prior to being gunned down, but he was not inexperienced, having held police posts in other cities for several years. Similarly, another chief had headed up his force only about a year before his murder, but he had 17 years prior police experience after seven years as a United States Marine. He was hardly inexperienced! On the other hand, two officers were inexperienced by any measure. One had only three months of service when he died from a shotgun wound suffered during an arrest attempt. Another had six months of service when he, too, was felled by a shotgun blast while attempting to make an arrest.

These data show that there is no correlation between one's years in law enforcement and one's safety. But what may be concluded from these figures is that an officer reaches peak exposure to criminal activity during the fifth or sixth year of service. This picture corresponds with FBI accounts of officer victimization, as well as with information derived from the Oklahoma University Police Assaults Study of over 1,100 incidents in 1973.

Military Service

Twenty-nine of the 61 victims had prior military experience, 22 had none, and there were ten officers for whom military service information could not be found. Veterans' military service ranged from World War I duty to several men who were combat veterans of World War II, Korea, and the Vietnamese war. Some were decorated veterans. None served in the Gulf War.

Educational Achievement

Information as to education was obtained for only 39 of the 61 officers. Three had earned bachelor's degrees, and 16 had been educated beyond high school, but had not earned a four-year degree. Seventeen were high school graduates with no subsequent education, while three did not complete high school. Not surprisingly, officers who were murdered from 1970 onward were more highly educated than persons victimized earlier.

Suspects

Many assumptions are made about cop killers. They are generally characterized as hardened, insensitive cold-blooded killers lacking any sense of compassion or guilt. They are often thought to be drug-crazed and to have long criminal records. The Oklahoma research reveals that by no means are these assumptions universally accurate.

When profiled, the 81 suspects resemble their 61 victims in but a few respects: the suspects were white males, born in Oklahoma, and lived in nonurban areas of the state. Not surprisingly, the suspects differed from their victims in many ways. They are about ten years younger, and they are by no means as well educated. Not all had jobs; those who did held blue collar jobs. Many of the suspects had been drinking, or were under the influence of alcohol or illegal drugs at the time of the incident. Finally, many, but by no means all, of the suspects had been arrested at least once prior to the fatal confrontation, and some had been in jail or prison prior to the incident. Five were jail or prison escapees, wanted by police. Several others were on parole or probation, while some were out on bail for earlier felonies, not related to the murder of an officer.

These are not surprising characteristics describing a group of persons who fight police. The exceptional thing is that the average age of a cop killer in Oklahoma is about eight years older than the average age of persons arrested for murder nationally.

By no means is there a clear-cut, easily identifiable type of person who murders police. The killer was not a primitive, animal-like breed of man or woman. Rather, the person was a truck or cab driver, a waitress, a laborer or a barber, among other things. Many were unemployed when they attacked an officer. The suspect may have had two or three semesters of college, or no formal education at all. He may be white, black or American Indian, and he may not be a he at all, but rather a female! All of this underscores that an officer should never be lulled into a sense of security, assuming that a suspect will offer no resistance.

Gender and Race

Almost all, 76 of 81, suspects were male. Of the males, 49 were white, 23 were black, and four were American Indian. Of the five females, two were black, two were white, and one was an American Indian.

Contrary to popular stereotype, most of the murder suspects were not black. Table 3.3 sets out the ethnicity of police officer murder suspects in Oklahoma and nationwide.

TABLE 3.3

THE ETHNICITY OF POLICE OFFICER MURDER SUSPECTS

Race	Oklahoma 1950-1994		Nationwide 1965-1994	
	Number	Percent	Number	Percent
White	51	63.0	1,899	52.2
Black	25	30.8	1,673	45.9
Other*	5	6.2	68	1.9
TOTAL	81	100.0	3,640	100.0

*Includes Asian/Pacific Islander and American Indian/Alaskan Native.

Of the 18,475 persons arrested nationally during 1994 for all types of murders, 41.7 percent were white, 56.4 percent were black, .7 percent were American Indian or Alaskan Native, and 1.2 percent were Asian or Pacific Islander. None of the national data about persons who murder police or who commit other classes of murder support the notion that blacks are cop killers, any more so than others.

Of the 31 suspects in the 20 urban murders, 15 were white, 15 were black, and there was one Indian female. Of the 50 suspects in the 41 nonurban murders, 34 were white males. There were nine black males and four male American Indian suspects in addition to three white female suspects involved in nonurban incidents.

Birthplace

Thirty-nine, or almost one of every two of the killers, were born in Oklahoma, while 42 were born in one of 16 other states. None were born outside the United States. The non-Oklahoman suspects were from Arizona, Arkansas, Colorado, California, Mississippi, Massachusetts, Missouri, Kansas, Indiana, New York, North Dakota, North Carolina, Ohio, Tennessee, Texas, and Virginia.

Two of the out-of-state suspects were AWOL servicemen, and one was an escaped convict from North Carolina. That only three of 42 suspects were from states west of Oklahoma suggests that there are few people who move to Oklahoma once they have savored the virtues of the nation's western slope!

Age

A national trend shows the overwhelming involvement of youth, 18 years of age and under, in crime. This failed to surface in the composite picture of the age of Oklahoma police officer murder suspects. In fact, the suspects were, generally speaking, between the ages of 20 and 29. The youngest suspect was 16; another was 17. The oldest were two white males, both 74. The average age of the 81 Oklahoma suspects was 30.5 years. The two 74-year-olds were both involved in nonurban incidents and both were killed at the scene. One of the suspects was reportedly suffering mental difficulties prior to the incident, while the other suddenly went berserk, endangering officers. The age ranges of the Oklahoma suspects is shown in Table 3.4. There are no comprehensive nationwide data about the age of persons suspected of killing police.

TABLE 3.4

THE NUMBER OF SUSPECTS BY AGE RANGES IN THE MURDER OF OKLAHOMA POLICE 1950 THROUGH 1994

Age Range	Number of Suspects	Percentage of Suspects in Range	Percentage of Oklahoma's 1990 Population in Range
0-14	—		22.3
15-19	6	7.4	7.4
20-24	26	32.0	7.2
25-29	22	27.2	7.9
30-34	7	8.6	8.3
35-39	5	6.2	7.6
40-44	5	6.2	6.8
45-49	2	2.5	5.6
50-54	2	2.5	4.7
55-59	2	2.5	4.5
60-64	1	1.2	4.3
65-69	1	1.2	4.2
70-74	2	2.5	3.3
75+	—	—	5.9
TOTALS	81	100.0	100.0

Educational Achievement

Educational achievement information was found for 49 of the suspects. While 15 suspects were high school graduates, the average level of schooling for all 49 suspects was about ten years, or sophomore level in high school. A black suspect was the most highly educated, having completed one and one-half years of college. Three urban and two rural suspects had one year of college. The least educated was the 69-year old black slayer of a black Ardmore police officer who, according to prison records, had received no formal education. Information about 20 of the 24 suspects involved in urban murders revealed that these men and women were slightly better educated than their rural counterparts. Their average level of education was that of a senior in high school, just short of high school graduation.

Occupation and Employment

Of the 81 suspects, 38 were employed at the time of the incident, 17 were unemployed, and the employment status of 14 suspects was unknown. Of the other 12 offenders, two were AWOL servicemen; two were retired; five were jail/prison escapees; two were students; and one was an unemployed disabled person. That several suspects were unemployed at the time of the murder matches a larger picture, wherein social scientists traditionally cite unemployment as contributing to anti-social behavior.

While the most common occupation of the suspects, when they held jobs, was that of laborer, there were a striking variety of other callings in which the persons toiled. These are shown in Table 3.5.

TABLE 3.5

OCCUPATIONS PURSUED BY PERSONS
WHO MURDERED OKLAHOMA POLICE
1950 THROUGH 1994

Truck/equipment driver	Warehouseman	Painter
Laborer	Boilermaker	Prize fighter
Farmer	Carpenter	Sales
Welder	Oil field machinist	School bus driver
Mechanic	Brick layer	Taxi cab driver
Barber	Crop duster pilot	Tree surgeon
Armed forces	Domestic worker	Trucking executive
Construction worker	Office clerk	Upholsterer
Electrician	Maid	Waitress

Alcohol and Other Drug Use

Alcohol consumption and the use of illegal drugs was prominent in the murder of Oklahoma officers. Although drug use itself cannot be labeled "the cause" of police slayings, it certainly contributes to the carnage. Through it, inhibitions are lessened. The short person, the young adult, the unemployed individual, the minority group member who perceives him or herself as enslaved, might feel threatened. When drugs reduce inhibitions, aggressive behavior may be directed toward others. In the Oklahoma study, the person seen as blocking opportunities was the police officer. His murder ensued.

It is certain that in 17 of the 59 incidents, suspects either had been drinking heavily or were under the influence of alcohol or illegal drugs. In about 25 other incidents, it appears very likely that suspects had consumed alcohol or some other drug immediately before the incident, but the level of intake was not able to be determined. What was certain was that in only 17 of the incidents, alcohol or other drugs were not factors in the slaying. These figures confirm that the relationship between drugs and assaults on police officers parallels the long-recognized relationship between drug abuse and violence.

Past Criminal History

What kind of a rap sheet did the persons who murdered Oklahoma lawmen have? Are police murderers hardened criminals with extensive arrest records, or are they small-time hoods, characters who are local nuisances, hardly deserving the title of criminal? Or were people who killed Oklahoma police like anyone else, except when they drank too much and killed an officer?

In order to find out who killed cops in Oklahoma, data were extracted from the criminal history records for 75 of the 81 suspects. In the six instances where there were no rap sheets, suspects were never fingerprinted. The authorities apparently felt that it was unnecessary and would serve no useful purpose, since five of the six either were killed by police at the time of the incident or committed suicide. The sixth, critically wounded during the incident, lived out his days in a state mental hospital.

When all the tallying is done and each of the 75 suspects' criminal history is put under a microscope, it is apparent that, as a group, these are disturbed people who got fogged up on alcohol or other drugs and ended up murdering police. Only seven of the 75 were what police would class as "heavies." Ten others showed signs of being violent and warranted great caution. These included one who was a fugitive felon from North Carolina, just passing through, and four others who were escapees from penal facilities in Oklahoma who, when faced by police, chose not to surrender. The other five had criminal histories that featured violence. Another 58 were, at worst, unskilled thieves or novice stickup men who bungled not-too-complicated heists.

Some suspects apparently suffered from mental aberrations and had befuddled their minds with alcohol or other drugs before the confrontation which took an officer's life. In short, the data disclose that the small time criminal, arrested once or twice for nonviolent crimes, was the person most likely to murder an Oklahoma police officer.

What Suspects Were Arrested For

As Table 3.6 shows, with some notable exceptions, most of the 75 suspects had little prior criminal history. In fact, the table shows that the suspects averaged 2.7 felony arrests each. Moreover, on only 153 occasions were the 75 suspects taken into police custody for misdemeanor, traffic, or other reasons.

TABLE 3.6

THE NUMBER OF PRIOR ARRESTS BY THE TYPE OF INCIDENT ATTRIBUTABLE TO 75 SUSPECTS IN THE SLAYING OF 61 OKLAHOMA LAWMEN, 1950 THROUGH 1994*

Type of Incident	Number of Incidents for Which Suspects Were Arrested	Actual Number of Suspects Arrested for the Type of Incident	Percent of the 75 Suspects Who Have Been Arrested by Type of Incident
Murder/Manslaughter	4	4	5.3
Rape/Molestation	5	5	6.7
Robbery	26	14	18.7
Aggravated Assault	17	12	16.0
Weapons Offenses	8	7	9.3
Burglary	44	26	34.7
Forgery/Checks/Counterfeiting	13	10	13.3
Grand Theft	18	13	17.3
Auto Theft	29	16	21.3
Narcotics-Distribution	13	9	12.0
Escape from Custody/Aiding	20	11	14.7
Other Felonies	9	8	10.7
TOTAL FELONIES:	206	Average Felonies per Suspect:	2.7
Simple Assault	4	3	4.0
Petty Theft	11	9	12.0
Hit and Run	2	2	2.7
DUI/DWI, other liquor	16	9	12.0
Narcotics-Possession	7	5	6.7
Vagrancy/Loitering	27	8	10.7
Disorderly Conduct/Drunk	24	17	22.7
Other Traffic	14	8	10.7
Other Misdemeanor	9	9	12.0
Resisting Arrest and Assault on an Officer	10	8	10.7
Investigation	16	11	14.7
Other/Unknown	13	9	12.0
TOTAL Misdemeanors and Other Incidents:	153	Average Misdemeanors per Suspect:	2.1
ARRESTS FOR SOME INCIDENT:	359	Average Arrests for Some Incident Per Suspect:	4.8

*Source: These data were extracted from federal and state criminal history records for each of the 75 suspects. Data shown in Tables have been derived from the same sources.

Surprisingly, 19 of the 75 suspects had never been arrested at all prior to murdering an officer. On the other extreme, one man, 24 years of age, had been arrested 37 times, 16 times for felony offenses, before he ended his career by murdering an Oklahoma City officer. A second suspect was on parole from California when an Oklahoma City officer intervened as the felon was holding up a fast food store. This parolee had at least 13 known earlier arrests for offenses ranging from murder, robbery, aggravated assault, burglary, car theft, child molestation, escape, and aiding and abetting an escapee, as well as smuggling firearms into a prison. The third "heavy" murdered a deputy sheriff and a citizen in Oklahoma's panhandle early one morning as the two investigated suspicious circumstances. This murderer had been arrested 12 times previously, eleven of these being for felonies. He and his co-killer were escapees from the Wagoner County jail in eastern Oklahoma at the time of the murders.

Burglary, seen as a crime of stealth, was the offense for which most police killers had been arrested before they took a lawman's life. This is not surprising, since of the seven Index Crimes set out by the FBI in its crime reporting program, burglary constitutes about 20 percent of the total crimes reported each year. But what makes the offense of burglary, supposedly a nonviolent crime, of such concern to police is that guns and ammunition are often taken. This means that even if burglars are not armed when they break into a place, police have reason to anticipate that they may have armed themselves while on the job.

In the misdemeanor category, arrests for vagrancy/loitering were the most common. A female murderer was the principal contributor to this category, as she had been arrested eleven times for vagrancy, owing to her activities as a prostitute in a southwestern Oklahoma town. The second highest category, disorderly conduct/drunkenness, accounted for 24 arrests. The number of arrests for these two classes of misdemeanors would be dramatically greater if drunkenness, vagrancy, and loitering hadn't been decriminalized many years ago.

Forty-nine of the 75 suspects had been arrested for a felony, several of them more than once. Only 44 of the 75 had been taken into custody for a misdemeanor charge.

The sum of arrests for violent crimes is modest. The 75 suspects totalled only four arrests for murder, five for rape and molestation, and 17 for aggravated assault. There were but eight arrests for weapons offenses, one of these being for smuggling firearms into prison, and only ten prior arrests for resisting arrest or assaulting an officer. There were four arrests for simple assault and one for train wrecking. While many of the 75 suspects had arrest records, by no means did they, as a group, have the kind of criminal background that would cause police officers to expect the violence and aggression associated with deadly assault.

Nationally, from 1964-1994, there were 3,358 persons identified in the killing of police officers, as shown in Table 3.7. Certain characteristics, unique to these persons, may be contrasted with the 75 Sooner State suspects. Far fewer Oklahoma suspects had pre-incident weapons law violations and narcotics arrests than the national group. On the other hand, Oklahoma suspects did slightly more cop fighting than the national group.

TABLE 3.7

A PROFILE OF PERSONS IDENTIFIED IN THE KILLING
OF POLICE OFFICERS IN OKLAHOMA 1950 THROUGH 1994
AND NATIONWIDE 1964 THROUGH 1994

Factor Unique to Persons Identified	Oklahoma		Nationally	
	Persons Identified	% of Total Persons Identified	Persons Identified	% of Total Persons Identified
Total Number of Persons Identified in Killings	75	100.0	3,358	100.0
Convicted on Prior Criminal Charges	56	74.7	2,476	73.7
Prior Arrest for Crime of Violence	30	40.0	1,369	40.8
On Parole or Probation at Time of Killing	6	8.0	710	21.1
Prior Arrest for Murder	4	4.0	164	4.9
Prior Arrest for Drug Law Violation	12	16.0	688	20.5
Prior Arrest for Assaulting an Officer or Resisting Arrest	9	12.0	354	10.5
Prior Arrest for Weapons Law Violation	8	10.7	999	29.7

Criminal history sheets disclose that only six of the 75 suspects, or 8.0 percent, were on probation or parole at the time they murdered an officer. A seventh suspect had recently completed his parole. Nationally, Table 3.7 shows that 21.1 percent of the persons identified in the murders of police officers were on parole or probation when an officer was killed. This comparison underscores the finding that persons who murdered Oklahoma lawmen were not, as a group, desperate career criminals, notwithstanding the fact that seven of the murderers were very, very seasoned, ugly criminals and five others were escapees at the time they killed a police officer.

Urban vs. Nonurban Arrest Patterns

Only seven of the 30 urban suspects had never been arrested, as compared with 12 nonurban suspects who had never been taken into custody prior to murdering an Oklahoma police officer. Twenty-one of 30 urban suspects and 27 of 45 nonurban suspects had prior arrests for one or more felony offenses. Seventeen of 30, and 29 of 45 non-urban suspects, had been arrested for one or more misdemeanor or other offenses.

Urban suspects had far heavier arrest records than their rural counterparts, having an average of 4.5 felony arrests per suspect. The nonurban suspects averaged 2.0 felony arrests per person, not an inconsequential number for country folk. The urban suspects topped their nonurban counterparts in misdemeanor and other arrests, too, averaging 2.7 per suspect in contrast to 2.1 for those from the state's less densely populated areas. Cumulatively, the urban suspects averaged 7.2 arrests, while the nonurban group averaged far fewer: 4.1 arrests per suspect.

There were some suspects whose extensive criminal records distorted the averages. For example, one urban suspect had one arrest for rape, two for robbery, one for aggravated assault, two each for weapons offenses, burglary, and plain drunk. The same man had been arrested eight times for auto theft, five for vagrancy/loitering, four for disorderly conduct, once each for resisting arrest and evading arrest, and twice each for escape from custody and assault on an officer. This totalled 37 arrests, 16 for felonies and 21 for misdemeanors. His criminal history, alone, accounts for 10.3 percent of all 359 arrests for all 75 suspects!

About Convictions

By no means does arrest automatically result in conviction. This is dramatically demonstrated in Table 3.8 which shows a summary of the arrests-convictions picture for the 75 felony suspects, and in Table 3.9 which shows misdemeanors. The tables show that well over one-half of all suspects have been convicted of either a felony or misdemeanor. As a group, these killers are not very experienced in the criminal justice system.

TABLE 3.8

TOTAL PRE-INCIDENT ARRESTS AND CONVICTIONS FOR FELONIES

Total Suspects	Number Having a Felony Arrest	Number Having a Felony Conviction
75	48	37

TABLE 3.9

TOTAL PRE-INCIDENT ARRESTS AND CONVICTIONS FOR MISDEMEANORS

Total Suspects	Number Having a Misdemeanor Arrest	Number Having a Misdemeanor Conviction
75	45	30

None of the four men, who had previously been arrested and convicted of murder, were among the two who were executed for murdering an Oklahoma lawman. One of the men with an earlier murder conviction, had only a single previous arrest—for drunk driving for which he was convicted, fined, and sentenced to the county jail. Another previous murderer had been arrested and convicted of aggravated assault and faced five prior misdemeanor charges, including two for drunk driving. He had been convicted following every arrest. The third murderer had twice been charged with and convicted of check offenses, which are not of an aggressive nature. The fourth person with a prior murder conviction had also been convicted 12 times, including four times for robbery, and one each for aggravated assault, burglary, car theft, child molestation, escape, and smuggling firearms into prison. Three of the previous murderers were from rural Oklahoma and their encounters with police were out in the country. The fourth was from Oklahoma City where he murdered an officer.

Convicted of murder, prior to killing the officer, how did the four suspects manage to get out of prison? One had been convicted of murder in Tulsa in 1919 and was sentenced to 20 years. Then he murdered an Ardmore police officer in 1958, well after expiration of the original sentence. Another suspect was sentenced to ten years in 1947 for manslaughter in Muskogee, but was released from McAlester Penitentiary in 1952. He murdered a Claremore police officer two years later and took his own life at the incident scene rather than submit to arrest. The third person was convicted of first degree manslaughter in 1975 and was doing 50 years in McAlester Penitentiary. He and a violent fellow inmate broke out of McAlester Penitentiary in May, 1978, and murdered three highway patrol personnel. The fourth person with a prior conviction for murder, was in violation of his parole for robbery in California. This man, seriously wounded shortly after killing an officer, committed suicide as he awaited trial.

A review of the prior records of the two men executed for murdering police is revealing. While each had been arrested, their offenses were not especially remarkable. One had been arrested for and convicted of resisting arrest, but he was never convicted following three arrests for burglary. The second murderer who was executed had been arrested on three prior occasions, once each for aggravated assault, plain drunk, and drunk driving, but he had never been convicted.

Chapter 4

FROM ARREST TO DISPOSITION

Once arrested, a suspect is subject to the procedural steps inherent in the justice process. These include arraignment, representation by counsel, bail, and at the suspect's option, a preliminary hearing. Then, assuming the suspect has not fallen out of the system for any of a number of reasons, there is the trial, and should there be a conviction, sentencing.

When a cop killer is arrested, police try to get the suspect to trial as soon as possible after the prosecutor has assembled the case. However, getting to trial often seems to proceed at a snail's pace, the process being snagged on procedural questions and motions. This is **delay**, and authorities generally believe the greater the delay, the less likely the chance of a conviction. Moreover, if it takes a long time to convict a suspect, there is concern that the sentence may not fit the severity of the act of killing an officer. Indeed, many police officers feel that, if cases take a long time from arrest to disposition, criminals get a sense that "nothing happens" to police killers. Delay, then, may encourage aggression against police. Conversely, if there is a quick capture and conviction, followed by a no-nonsense penalty, attacks on police may be reduced because of the evidence that society supports its lawmen.

While judicial proceedings were no issue to the 14 Oklahoma cop killers who were slain by police or took their own lives, 67 others were arrested and faced the criminal justice process. The offenses with which they were charged, and the outcomes, are shown in Table 4.1.

TABLE 4.1

THE NATURE OF THE CHARGE AND OUTCOME FOR
SIXTY-SEVEN MURDER SUSPECTS

Charge	Number Charged	Verdict / Outcome	
Murder in the first degree	62		43
Murder in the second degree	2		3
First degree manslaughter	2		6
Second degree manslaughter	1		1
		Plea bargain to robbery	1
		Charges dismissed	8
		Acquitted	2
		Died or killed before trial	3
Total	67		67

Getting to Trial

While there are as many delays in Oklahoma criminal cases as there are in any other state, almost all Oklahoma police officer murder suspects were processed from arrest through trial with relative speed. In fact, 48 of the 54 suspects who were sentenced after trial were sentenced within one year of the incident! Moreover, speed did not compromise the suspects' right to due process because only two of the 54 convictions were later overturned by the Oklahoma Court of Criminal Appeals.

The shortest time from the incident to sentencing was 34 days, a case in which an AWOL airman pleaded guilty to murdering a sheriff's deputy. The most expeditious processing of a suspect who pleaded not guilty and went to trial took 58 days from the incident to sentencing.

There were six suspects whose cases did not get to trial within a year of the incident. By comparison, 21 were sentenced within six months of the murder. Even in the case of the suspect arrested 198 days after the incident, the entire proceeding was concluded within 270 days of the murder. This suspect was arraigned on the day of his arrest, his preliminary hearing was 22 days later, and his trial was convened 39 days after that. The trial lasted two days, resulting in the suspect's conviction. He was sentenced nine days after the verdict was entered, and transported to prison eleven days later.

The speed with which these cases were processed not only speaks well of the judicial branch which heard the cases, but also points to excellent police investigatory work, which located the suspects so soon after the homicide. And it commends the prosecutorial staffs, too, for being trial-ready so promptly.

Certain characteristics which mark the various steps in the criminal justice process in every state are now described as pertains to the Oklahoma murder suspects.

Plea Bargaining

While there were a few occasions where prosecutors negotiated pleas with murder suspects, there were not many. When a bargain was struck, it was the product of a weak evidentiary case, or one suspect's testimony was needed against another. It is rare, however, to see a negotiated plea in cases of police killings, as the prosecutor may face public criticism if he or she bargains out in an especially heinous case. Cop killer trials are almost always widely reported by the media, so the conduct of the prosecutor is highly visible. From the time of arrest to arraignment, both prosecutors and defense attorneys go about assembling the evidence needed to present their cases. Of course, there will be time for further case preparation, all the way up to trial, which may be several months later.

Representation by Counsel

Many citizens believe that cop killers neither need nor deserve representation by counsel. They see these cases as open and shut and feel that counsel is unnecessary, a frill of our judicial process. Others sharply disagree, saying that when the death penalty, or the possibility of a life sentence exists, legal representation is imperative and is constitutionally guaranteed by the Bill of Rights. The United States Supreme Court supports this position.

Of the 67 suspects who entered Oklahoma's criminal justice system, at least 65 were represented by counsel, either an attorney hand-picked by the defendant, or a court-appointed lawyer. The documentation is insufficient to determine whether the other two cop killers were represented, but almost certainly they were.

It is the job of counsel to assure that the accused is afforded due process and to pick apart the police investigatory work, which must be impeccably documented from the moment the case first breaks, until the trial. While the guilty verdicts in Oklahoma underscore the excellence of the police investigations and the pretrial preparation by the prosecution, by no means do they reflect a lack of skill on the part of defense counsel. The factual circumstances of almost every case show that it was overwhelming evidence, not inept defense counsel, which led to the suspect's conviction. Attorneys for the defense, distasteful as they may be to some persons, are a critical component of our criminal justice system.

The belief that privately retained counsel was more effective than court appointed counsel in defending a suspect was not borne out in Oklahoma. Neither was the stereotype that a cop killer is an impoverished, embattled criminal, unable to afford an attorney. The data reveal that about one of every three suspects was represented by retained, rather than court-appointed, counsel.

Bail

A view widely held is that people suspected of killing police officers are too dangerous to be allowed back on the streets. The tough bail requirements, set by the court, and the frequency with which bail is denied, seem to reflect this. High bail, or its denial, and the suspects' inability to post it, result in a long period of incarceration before trial for most police murder suspects.

The purpose of bail is to insure that a suspect will be present for trial. Some of the points a judge takes into consideration, when reaching a bail judgment, include the severity of the crime, the suspect's ties to the community, whether or not he or she might flee, the danger the suspect would pose to society if released on bail, family and employment status, prior criminal history, and one's parole or probation history. The bail decision in cop killing cases attracts public scrutiny, as cop killing is a high profile matter.

Once booked into jail, suspects are interested in the terms of their bail, or bond as it is sometimes called. For some serious offenses, a judge is not required to set bail. Since murder in the first degree is one of these, it is not surprising that 53 of the 67 suspects were denied bail. Bail was set on eleven of the suspects, and three others, two males and one female, were released on their personal recognizance. Of the eleven prisoners, only seven actually posted bail and were released pending hearings and trial.

The seven suspects who posted bail included two males charged with manslaughter in the death of an Oklahoma City officer, both released on $5,000 bail. In an Ardmore case, a 69-year-old suspect was released on $500 bail, the lowest amount set for any of the killers. He was in failing health and was so debilitated that he posed no danger to anyone, a crucial factor in the judge's decision. Two other cop killers were disallowed bail because they were considered likely to be very dangerous. However, in these two cases bail was later allowed by the Court of Criminal Appeals and it was posted, to the dismay of authorities.

Arrest to Arraignment

Once a suspect is arrested, due process requires that he or she be taken, as soon as possible, before a magistrate to be informed of the charges. This is termed an initial appearance. It is at this point that arrangements for counsel are made, including the appointment of counsel if the suspect is unable to afford an attorney. A bail decision may be made at this time, although the committing magistrate may not do so until the accused has counsel and has entered a plea to the charges. Finally, if the proceedings go according to form, the judge will set a date for arraignment.

The average time between arrest and arraignment was just over one month. On the expeditious side, one suspect was arraigned on the day of his arrest, and two were arraigned one day after their arrest. The longest time between arrest and arraignment was for two suspects in a 1960 murder of an Ardmore officer, about 400 days each. A third suspect in that case spent 324 days in jail before his arraignment. In the late 1990s, such a delay would almost certainly be grounds for reversible error, should there be a conviction at the subsequent trial. Significantly, the average time from arrest to arraignment was distorted by these three suspects. Without including them, that time shrinks to 18 days.

The Preliminary Hearing to Trial

Forty-nine suspects requested a preliminary hearing; eleven others waived their privilege and were bound over for trial. The data fail to disclose whether seven other suspects had such a hearing.

The preliminary hearing, which is a judicial hearing intended to determine if there is probable cause to bind a suspect over for trial on the charge, is not a constitutionally guaranteed right. Rather, it is an optional step which allows the defense to discover the nature and extent of the state's evidence which may help the suspect's attorney prepare for the trial. It is also an opportunity for defense counsel to catch the state's witnesses unprepared, should the prosecutor be lazy, getting imperfect testimony on the record. The fact that 49 suspects opted to have a preliminary hearing indicates the desire of the accused, through counsel, to get an early reading on the chances for acquittal or to attempt to reach a negotiated plea.

All 49 suspects were bound over. An average of almost 135 days elapsed between the preliminary hearings and the trial. In one case the trial began only five days after the preliminary hearing; the longest time was nearly a year, 322 days.

Dismissed Charges

That eight suspects had charges against them dismissed seems unusual, since the dismissal of cop killing charges is not readily agreed to by a prosecuting attorney. When it does happen, the dismissal order is almost surely based on unique circumstances which the prosecutor may quickly explain. The eight dismissals, related below, illustrate some typical, but understandable, circumstances which prompted charges to be dropped.

Two suspects, who were involved in a 1954 brawl, had charges of manslaughter against them dismissed. The murder occurred when an Oklahoma City officer and his partner were quelling an early morning family disturbance which had spilled out of a bar onto the center parkway strip on an arterial street. An officer was attempting to separate a husband and wife who were fighting when he was pulled to the ground by the husband. The husband allegedly attempted to withdraw the officer's gun from its holster, which prompted his partner to draw his own weapon. At this point in the melee there was a gunshot. The slug killed the officer that was involved in the scuffle. The husband and wife were arrested and charged, as it was believed that one of them had fired the fatal shot. However, further investigation showed that the other officer's gun had discharged accidentally when he had used it to strike one of the combatants.

Another dismissal also took place in Oklahoma City. In this case, one suspect agreed to testify against his accomplices and the murder charge against him was dismissed. Similar circumstances brought about the dismissal of charges against one of two suspects in the 1982 murder of a Spencer officer, and in the 1985 murder of an Oklahoma City officer. In none of these cases was the person who gave testimony for the state the triggerman.

A mistrial in one case and a hung jury in the second resulted in the dismissal of charges against one suspect in the murder of a town marshal. It was unlikely that a jury would find him guilty, so it precluded a third trial. The seventh and eighth persons who were released from charges were found to have had no role whatsoever in the two murders.

Length of the Trial

The longest of the 39 trials was 24 days. The suspect was found not guilty by reason of insanity and committed to a state mental institution. Two other trials, both of urban suspects, lasted 16 and 15 days, respectively. Eight of the 34 trials were started and finished on the same day. In two of the cases the jury deliberated for only 30 minutes before returning a verdict! The average length of all trials over the 45-year span is five days.

Trials are definitely getting longer and more complicated. For example, the trials from 1950 through 1974 averaged 3.4 days duration. Trials in the last 20 years averaged eleven days.

Several of the suspects, because of mistrials or higher court rulings, were tried more than once, and a few suspects were tried for more than one murder.

Post-Conviction Maneuvers

Appeals and other post-conviction legal maneuvers are not uncommon. These processes, though costly and judicially time-consuming, are not difficult for a convicted prisoner to file, owing to easy access to free legal counsel and law libraries. Some become known as pretty good jailhouse lawyers. However, the record shows that Oklahoma cop killers have had little success with their post-conviction gyrations.

Acquittals

There were two acquittals: one by reason of insanity, and in the other, the jury believed that the suspect shot the officer in self-defense.

Time From Arrest to Sentencing

The criminal justice process grinds ahead slowly, but deliberately, in cop killings. In fact, it seems to be progressively slowing down: from 1950 through 1984, suspects spent an average of 167 days in jail from arrest to sentencing in the Oklahoma cases. In the past decade, 1985 through 1994, suspects spent an average of 268 days from arrest to sentencing. While a few suspects languished in jail between arrest and the outcome of the trial, no Oklahoma convictions were overturned on appeal on the basis of unreasonable delay.

Manslaughter Convictions

In homicide cases in Oklahoma, the judge must, also, instruct the jury as to the lesser offenses of homicide. These include second degree murder, first and second degree manslaughter, and involuntary manslaughter. The jury then must decide which charge to convict upon, appropriate to the evidence introduced. This accounts for seven suspects being convicted of a lesser charge than first degree murder, which was sought by the prosecution.

Sentences of from five to 100 years were imposed on six killers following convictions for first degree manslaughter. A seventh person, charged with and convicted of second degree manslaughter, was sentenced to one year in jail and was fined $1,000. This suspect could have been sentenced to serve from two to four years in the Oklahoma State Penitentiary, but the evidence strongly suggested that he killed the officer unintentionally.

The six persons convicted of first degree manslaughter were originally charged with first degree murder. However, the complications of second and third trials, when the first trial had been reversed on appeal, may have caused the subsequent trials to result in conviction on lesser charges.

A tactical consideration may prompt a district attorney to seek a manslaughter conviction rather than risking acquittal on a murder charge. A 1973 case, where an officer was murdered by a prisoner in his custody, is a good example of an appeals court opinion having influenced the course of a second trial. In the first trial, the suspect was convicted of murder and sentenced to life imprisonment. However, a psychiatrist with the State Department of Mental Health was allowed to testify about conversations, after the arrest, between the suspect and the psychiatrist which, in effect, were confessions of the crime. The Oklahoma Court of Criminal Appeals determined that this testimony was inadmissible because it was derived from a doctor-patient confidential relationship. The conviction was reversed and the case was remanded, the psychiatrist's testimony being disallowed at the second trial. The loss of this testimony forced the prosecutor to seek a conviction for first degree manslaughter.

Sentences, Including the Death Penalty

Thirty-six of the 54 persons whose guilt was established were found guilty following trial by jury. Eighteen suspects pleaded guilty. Sentences imposed on the 54 persons, 51 men and three women, are shown in Table 4.2.

TABLE 4.2

SENTENCES ASSESSED TO FIFTY-FOUR SUSPECTS

Sentence	Number of Persons
Death	8
Imprisonment for life	35
100 years	1
65 years	1
40 years	3
20 years	1
4 to 20 years	1
8 years	1
5 years	2
1 year in county jail and $1,000 fine	1
Total	**54**

Summary

With few exceptions, persons who murder police officers in Oklahoma pay a stiff price for their act. That 43 suspects were sentenced to life in prison, or execution, underscores the public attitude toward this class of offender. The surprise is that so few suspects, only eight, were sentenced to death, and only two executed! Both executions stemmed from murders committed well before the July, 1972, *Furman vs. Georgia* United States Supreme Court decision which, for several years, effectively put capital punishment on hold across the nation. These killers were put to death in 1956 and 1960, 445 and 609 days, respectively, after they murdered police.

PART III

WHAT TO DO ABOUT ATTACKS ON POLICE

A natural reaction to Parts I and II of this book is the nagging question, "What could have been done to prevent the murder of these law enforcement officers?" The effects of these deaths upon the families, colleagues, and police agencies are irreversible, but the losses can be given value by learning from the experiences and using that knowledge to devise means to prevent future line-of-duty killings, where possible.

Part 3 offers clues which might reduce the risks faced by law enforcement officers. It is based on research, set out earlier, which has identified the circumstances under which killings occurred, the mechanisms used to kill, and information about the killers. While enlightening, it does not support definitive conclusions, and does not yield sufficient insight to guarantee preventive measures. Nevertheless, the research enhances the ability of law enforcement leaders, officers, and scholars to make objective observations, draw conclusions supported by fact, and make educated inferences about the probable success of proposed preventive measures. When considering possible remedies and countermeasures, however, five factors are important.

First, it is apparent that some attacks on police are, in fact, attacks against governmental authority targeting the government's most readily accessible and visible representatives, who are law enforcement personnel. As long as a large segment of our society remains economically isolated and feels it is disenfranchised, this type of attack is likely to continue. If the number of poverty-stricken, undereducated individuals continues to grow, so will the likelihood of attack.

Second, as assaults on police continue to escalate in number and ferocity due to the availability of more deadly weapons and ammunition, the public and legislators have responded with tough new laws. Such laws, including the controversial "three strikes and you're out" law, are intended to improve the criminal justice system by harshly punishing offenders while deterring others from such acts. Vigilance must be maintained to ensure that these measures, however well-intentioned, are not so draconian that they undermine law enforcement by creating an oppressive environment intolerable to the general population. Of particular concern are laws which erode constitutional protections or diminish due process responsibilities of police officers. The judiciary will continue to be crucial in assuring that neither excesses against or by police will be tolerated.

Third, law enforcement needs to foster, support, and actively participate in academic and medical research directed at identifying causal factors for criminality, including attacks on police. As a rule, law enforcement has not been very enthusiastic about cooperating with external researchers, often being suspicious of them and considering such efforts to be counter-productive. However, finite resources must be used in the most effective and efficient manner. The growing implementation of community-oriented policing has recognized that police efforts are only a part of the much larger and more complicated whole. Law enforcement needs to cooperate with government, academia, medicine, and other professionals in a coherent attempt to acquire more insight into the criminal mind.

Fourth, all concerned must recognize that attacks on law enforcement are going to continue into the foreseeable future. Since violence and its triggering mechanisms are very difficult to predict, caution and vigilance on the part of police are critical components in planning and implementing all law enforcement activities.

In conclusion, numerous groups must collaborate to devise a program to prevent assaults on law enforcement officers. This partnership includes law enforcement and the people who train them: the United States Congress, and state and local legislative bodies, professional organizations, police departments and associations and unions, higher education and private research foundations, and civic groups.

Broadly, casualty reduction measures should include action in the following arenas: (1) improving training in both content and venue, taking full advantage of available research and technology; (2) adjusting departmental policies and procedures, acknowledging and incorporating rapidly evolving changes in both; (3) improving equipment and placing the best in the hands of officers performing field duties; (4) making jailing and undercover roles less dangerous; (5) passing new and amended laws; (6) capitalizing on treatment programs for violent offenders, including substance abuse treatment; (7) reducing societal tolerance of violence; and (8) conducting applied research.

Chapter 5

WHAT OFFICERS NEED TO KNOW: IMPROVING POLICE TRAINING

Because training is the single most important factor in preventing an officer from becoming a statistic, police should be trained to perform with efficiency, safety, and ease, and in accordance with the law and departmental procedures. Since President Johnson's National Crime Commission reported in 1967, almost all police in the United States are trained. However, the expected level of proficiency and the sophistication of training varies widely in spite of the implementation of peace officer training commissions and mandatory training standards laws in most states. You can never overtrain police; it is undertraining that has led to the victimization of officers. It is like the Bible says, "My people are destroyed for lack of knowledge" (Hosea 4:6).

Training, a very broad term, means much more than the instruction provided in the police academy. It includes the regular retraining or in service training of both veteran personnel and less experienced officers, the command training of supervisors, and training at the executive level. The goal of training should be to provide police, at all levels, with the skills required to execute their duties legally and to survive on the street.

In 1951, as a rookie officer with the Berkeley, California Police Department, I underwent what was then recognized as one of the most advanced training programs in the country. The program was designed to teach knowledge-based objectives such as the laws of arrest, search, and seizure; interview and interrogation, jail procedures, departmental rules, regulations and procedures, and guidelines for conducting preliminary criminal investigations.

NOTE: This chapter was co-authored by Dr. Carolyn H. Chapman of the College of Education, the University of Nevada, Reno.

In addition to the knowledge objectives, Berkeley's recruits were afforded substantial skills training, such as typewriting, firing on the range, operating emergency vehicles, taking field notes, and writing reports. The intended outcome was for trainees to acquire proficiency in skills like these.

The instruction provided to achieve both knowledge and skill outcomes in 1951 consisted of 160 hours of training, given over four intensive weeks. Most of it was devoted to listening to experienced officers deliver lectures, tell stories, and relate anecdotes. Some time was scheduled at the target range, where trainees practiced handling their weapons and increased their accuracy by shooting at targets. Shooting proficiency was assessed by calculating the percent of shots which struck the torso design on the targets. The only other skill training of any sort which was graded was typing which, interestingly, was given for 19 hours, or 12 percent, of the 160-hour training program. Other than being scored on the range and in typing, there were neither written exams on the knowledge conveyed by the trainers, nor were there minimum standards of proficiency which recruits had to achieve. When trainees had completed the four weeks of instruction, most of which was "seat time," they hit the street, as trained officers, who, understandably, worked under close supervision for the next several months. This was a form of training, too, because sergeants would thoroughly critique young officers at the conclusion of each investigation.

Evolving Curriculum

When professionals plan a curriculum, they identify the knowledge, skills, and attitudes intended as outcomes of any educational program. While the curriculum for preparing Berkeley police officers almost half a century ago focused primarily on the knowledge officers needed, with some attention to skills, today's curriculum for preparing law enforcement officers has evolved due to a rapidly expanding knowledge base and increased recognition of the complex skills and attitudes officers need to perform effectively in contemporary society. Today, not only has the curriculum evolved to include a broader range of outcomes, the instructional methods and materials for achieving these outcomes has changed dramatically. Emerging instructional technology of incredible sorts has enabled training programs to anticipate outcomes which were only dreamed of by our predecessors.

We will first examine the changes in **curriculum**—*what* officers need to know, especially in relation to preventing police injury or fatality—and then, at the end of this chapter, we will describe changes in **instruction**—*how* these outcomes can be attained, using newer instructional approaches and the latest technology.

Knowledge Essential to Officer Survival

Much of the knowledge needed years ago is still relevant, as officers still need to know the penal and traffic codes, the laws of arrest, search and seizure, departmental rules, regulations and procedures, report writing, and how to operate police equipment of all sorts. In addition, today's police officers need a wide range of knowledge that was not historically part of the training curriculum. To perform effectively today, officers need to understand behavioral sciences such as psychology and sociology, understand the increasingly diverse cultures of our society, and comprehend the unique behaviors and communication patterns which have been evolved by gangs and prison inmates.

BEHAVIORAL SCIENCE. Today, instruction in psychology, sociology and human relations is routine in many, but not all, police academies. At the very minimum, all law enforcement cadets should receive an introductory course in the behavioral sciences. On the street, the ability to recognize different attitudes towards police, and then anticipate impending violent behavior with a reasonable degree of accuracy, is invaluable. Departments should view classes teaching psychological profiles as a major step in alerting the law enforcement officer to the dangers found in the profession.

Ongoing instruction, in the psychological makeup of suspects and the general public, should be continued throughout each officer's career. Even season personnel can benefit from periodic training or refresher courses conducted by psychiatrists, sociologists, and criminologists from nearby universities. Additionally, specialized seminars for a region, with expert presenters from the FBI or the RCMP, are often available to smaller municipal departments across the United States and Canada.

Ideally, workshops could draw a group of police officers together with a behavioral scientist, or another specialist, as the discussion leader. These sessions promise to be lively, especially if officers have completed pertinent reading assignments and class preparation. Discussion would center on how the frightened or panicked citizen looks upon police, how suspects and criminals view police, and how the officer personally perceives his or her role. This atmosphere can be most beneficial to officers who may tend to over-simplify or see only one side to a situation. The capacity to sense and anticipate mindsets and attitudes helps patrol officers better prepare for sudden violence and aggressive behavior.

Furthermore, administrators could encourage psychologists, sociologists and psychiatrists to ride along with patrol officers to see what the street is really like. These mental health professionals could get a no-holds-barred perspective of violence, mental instability, and social conflict to augment their textbook and institutional experiences. Such experiences could help them develop more realistic, creative training activities. And patrol officers could enhance their understanding of the causes, personalities, and traits that underpin anti-social human behavior as they ride with such professionals.

READING BODY LANGUAGE. Knowing about body language is an aspect of behavioral science instruction that can be particularly useful to police officers. Making the decision to arrest is one thing; effecting it peacefully is another. Voice and bearing are crucial to controlling the suspect. But there is an additional element which police need to understand if they are to maintain the peace and assure safety. Officers need to be able to read and interpret the body language of every contact, whether the person seems to be a crime victim, a witness, or a suspect.

For years, social scientists and doctors have been refining intriguing concepts, derived from the studies of psychology and physiology. These concepts attempt to describe and explain the human behavior police officers so often encounter on the street. Julius Fast, in his book, *Body Language*, and Robert Ardrey in *The Territorial Imperative*, have done police a vast service by setting out the science of "kinesics." The theory is not only valuable to patrol officers, but to police interrogators as they go about their work. A recent book, *Principles of Kinesic Interview and Interrogation*, by Stan B. Walters, gives additional insight into how one might spot lies and get to the truth when questioning suspects, victims, witnesses, and informants.

The scientifically researched theory of kinesics asserts that a person's body "talks." With that knowledge, the alert and trained patrol officer may be able to read or otherwise sense what action might come next, by noting what the person is "saying" by means of nonverbal communication. Body language, coupled with verbal outpourings, signs of alcohol or drug consumption, and the physical surroundings, can serve as a crystal ball into the suspect's thoughts. Modern police training should include significant instruction to help officers interpret body language, as well as help officers control and adjust their own demeanor for best results in dealing with the public.

Here is an example of a problem familiar to all police. An officer, after telling a suspect that he or she is under arrest, is cursed and verbally abused by a noncompliant person. Annoyed, the officer places a hand on the suspect's shoulder and eases him or her towards the squad car. Almost instinctively, in response to the hand on the shoulder, the suspect suddenly swings on the officer.

The suspect is responding aggressively to an invasion of his or her personal space. Violence follows, perhaps prolonged and leading to injury. The predictability of this transaction should be understood by every officer. By exploring alternative methods for getting the suspect to the car, many potentially violent situations can be defused. Clearly, this type of arrest is highly dependent on the mental state of the suspect. For example, a wanted felon, knowing that capture will result in more prison time, is not likely to go with a cop, easily or willingly, under any conditions.

UNDERSTANDING DIVERSE CULTURES. Today, more than ever, police need some highly specific diversity training and education. It should be aimed at attacking preconceived negative attitudes and stereotypical thinking on the part of officers, a condition often traced to a lack of knowledge or misinformation as well as cynicism. These sessions should aim to make officers more aware of the unique characteristics of the various populations within their community. By sensitizing officers to the cultural differences among prominent minority groups, many incorrect assumptions might be prevented. Such steps can help ease racial, cultural and socio-economic tension, antagonism, and suspicion. This knowledge may, also, contribute to officer safety, since law enforcement personnel will have a better grasp of what to anticipate from people with different cultural mores.

It is not difficult to identify words and phrases which arouse instant animosity and hatred from specific minority groups and to insist that police avoid such words. But other signals are more subtle, and hence more difficult to deal with in a training sense. For example, if an officer has prolonged eye contact with a person who is Samoan, the Samoan accepts this as a challenge to fight. On the other hand, American Indians and persons of Mexican extraction may lower their eyes when an officer looks at them, which in these cultures is a sign of respect for authority. The officer may incorrectly interpret failure to look them in the eye as an indication that the person is being deceitful, untruthful, or showing signs of guilt. Also, police must understand that part of black culture is the predisposition for youths and young adults, both male and female, to just hang around, on the street, in groups. This causes officers a substantial unease when they are unaware that this is normal among such people. It can easily lead to unnecessary trouble and confrontation. Another hot button issue is that persons from the Pacific Rim nations object to being categorized as "Asians," because they know that there are hundreds of major ethnic groups in that massive area, each with unique cultures and standards of behavior. Unwittingly, police may offend these people, though their intentions are of the highest order.

GANG AND PRISON TALK, TATTOOS AND PRISON GAMES. Street gangs are famous for their colors, such as the red and blue worn by members of the Bloods and Crips, and gang graffiti, which defaces public and private property. Such symbols, called "marks" and "tags" by the gang members, are a way of communicating, designating territory, and warning off rival gangs. The drive-by shootings of one another, and innocent people, have become prominent examples of severe problems in our society. Gang bangers and wannabees, the low status members who stridently work to gain position, can be very dangerous for police. They have been known to provoke an officer into chasing after them into an isolated area or an alley. When the suspect car stops, a second gang car pulls in, boxing the police car, at which time gang bangers commence shooting.

Gang communications are not easy to second guess, as they are ever-changing. If, for some reason, one means of showing their affiliation or communicating is no longer an option, they will find another, which could be something as subtle as all members of the gang tieing their shoes the same way. Corrections employees must stay alert for any subtle change in appearance or behavior among the inmates, too.

The other highly publicized type of gang is composed of outlaw bikers. The most famous such gang is the Hell's Angels, whose organization and discipline are legendary. For instance, near Vancouver,

British Columbia, where the Angels have a strong presence, the power structure is comprised of the wannabees and the real leaders. The wannabees are the overweight, tattooed, nasty thugs portrayed on the movie screen as drug runners, enforcers, and hit men. The real leaders are likely to wear neckties and decent clothing, and would blend in with a group of business people. To the casual observer, they appear to be entrepreneurs, running restaurants, car repair shops, motorcycle shops, massage parlors, or booking agencies that supply exotic dancers. In the Hell's Angels, any gang member wannabee who tries to rise too quickly, without paying his dues, will be dealt with severely.

Convicts in penitentiaries, many of whom are from street gangs, supremacist groups, and biker gangs, have their own language, a special jargon understood in their world. It can be communication by words, handsignals, tattoos, or any other means they find effective. Since most hardened felons do county or municipal lockup time, at least while awaiting trial, inmates on the local level also learn con-talk, or find out how to tattoo themselves to look like "badasses." Such communication, so prevalent on the inside, is unintelligible, and therefore often unheard and unseen by the untutored ear or eye. However, if truth be known, it may be more understandable to the average person today than it was a decade ago. That is the result of the large influx of gang-bangers into the prison population, and their hip-hop and street-talk vocabularies arrive with them. This dialect, commonly heard on television, in movies and rap music, has melded with con-lingo, creating an ever-evolving prison language.

The syntax is hard to duplicate, but the words that follow give an example of today's merging of vocabularies: "I'm in all day. The C.O., she put a fish by my crib. The basehead had dead presidents, a piece and was trying to score some more crank. He flipped and ended up buckin' the man. A narc, packin' a 9, busted him in the hood." Translated, this means: "I'm in for life. The corrections officer, she put a new inmate by my cell. The coke addict had cash, a handgun and he was trying buy some more crack cocaine mixed with amphetamines. He got real crazy and ended up shooting at the police. A drug enforcement officer, carrying a 9mm handgun, arrested him in the neighborhood."

Knowledge of such con-lingo is indispensable to corrections personnel, whether they are working in federal, state or county penal facilities. Prisoners, if their slang is not understood, can secretly hatch escape plots, set up murders, instigate insurrections, and plan other criminal activities. Cons often use jargon as a means to test and determine whether the correctional staff is "in touch." Jail staff, if familiar with prison-speak, can respond with a suitable remark, to stay even with or one step ahead of the cons. In any event, untranslated jail jargon is a hazard to corrections officials.

The corrections staff is not the only group threatened and vulnerable when prison jargon is allowed to proliferate. Street cops, and detectives, too, have regular contact with convicts and ex-cons and should be as knowledgeable as possible in con-speak.

Prior knowledge of con-talk, and the ability to identify tattoos, may allow an officer to quickly distinguish a suspect as a former con, or at least as a person who has had experience with the juvenile or adult criminal justice system. When such an identification is quickly made, the officer has the advantage and may take precautions which seem consistent with the contact. If police better understand con-talk and the origin and meaning of tattoos, an officer should be able to work with a greater degree of safety.

One way to help police learn con-talk would be to have a knowledgeable corrections officer serve as a lexicographer. This person, skilled in "jargonese," would keep prison staff, as well as local police, up to date on the meaning of ever-changing con-and drug-talk common to a region. The same surveillance techniques are needed for sorting out the latest tattoos and prison games, which are not really "games" at all, but a cruel form of human manipulation perpetrated against penitentiary employees, other inmates, and the general public. One thing to keep in mind is that jargon and tattoos may be specific to certain areas depending on the ethnic origins of the inmates and the nature of the gangs, so one lexicographer may not be in touch with the jargon of other areas.

Periodic group discussions and presentations, training bulletins, and video documentaries could be utilized to disseminate relevant and timely information. A recent and important means of communication is the Internet. John Evans, an Edmonton, Alberta police officer and founder of "CopNet," utilized by police officers from around the world, says that law enforcement needs to utilize the World Wide Web more, for its own informational purposes. He says, "every crime conceivable is being committed by computer, including murder, robbery, theft, embezzlement, and fraud. If forces do not move soon, the Information Super Highway will become a no-go zone that is wide-open to criminal exploitation." It is evident that the Internet could very effectively serve law enforcement personnel to disseminate vital information to local forces, including information about gang activities and prison communications.

Penitentiary staff should learn how to recognize, stop, and prevent dangerous prison games. Employees and guards need to be able to spot the signs that a game is being set up, then decide which tactics are best suited to quashing it. Simply stated, convicts, sometimes working in groups or as good guy/bad guy, will try to gain the favor of a prison employee. Cons may try to persuade the officer to sneak in extra food, smokes, or even to make contact with a relative back home. It starts with modest demands, but culminates with the officer in a seriously compromised position, which could lead to being arrested or fired. Usually, cons try to use this serious dilemma as a way to blackmail staff into an illegal act such as supplying drugs, weapons, or other contraband. Or they may try to coerce an institutional employee, often a woman, into a sexual relationship. In one case, an inexperienced male corrections officer took pity on a friendly inmate's family and naively, and against prison policy, agreed to visit them at the family home. By doing so, he allowed himself to be set up, for soon after the visit, the "friendly" inmate produced secret photos showing the guard embracing the felon's young, attractive, and partially-clad wife. Ultimately, the corrections officer was fired, but not before he was seriously wounded by the "friendly" inmate, who was wielding a contraband knife.

History shows that when convicts try to set up games, they prey upon the guards with whom they feel they can most likely establish a sympathetic relationship. The first step is usually an effort by the convict to get on a first-name basis with the officer, a step which must be strongly resisted. Additionally, some inmates with access to telephones, will attempt to sucker or coerce the public into their illegal schemes, using ex-cons and unscrupulous buddies on the outside as intimidators, enforcers, and general purpose "muscle." And, of course, weaker inmates are often victimized by prison games and also used for sexual purposes.

Tattooing is seen by many as the last frontier of personal expression, as an art form. But in prison, tattoos are common among felons and may convey a significant meaning: a gang-banger, a cop killer, a skinhead, an outlaw biker, or an occultist. Many tattoos, adorning inmates and hoods, are unlike those one would contract for at a tattoo parlor. Prison tattoos, more often than not, are slashes, burns, or ink from a pen, injected under the skin with a crude prison-made tattoo gun. This self inflicted carnage usually results in extensive scar tissue.

Typical themes are prison names, gang signs on the arm, tear drops above the eyes, and marks showing the number of gang members or police killed. One popular tattoo consists of three dots on the hand indicating that a young offender has spent time in "juvie."

Watching out for distinctive tattoos can save an officer's life. A tattoo that says "Dead Cops" should put any law enforcement officer on high alert. Another tattoo is old, but still highly relevant to police. In the early 1980s, about 25,000 of the 125,000 refugees who flooded the United States from the Cuban port of Mariel, were hardened criminals, purposely shunted to the United States by Dictator Fidel Castro. They could be identified, if one knew what to look for: the Cuban government's incarceration tattoo, usually stamped between the thumb and index finger of the left hand.

The Marielitas have no monopoly on tattooing as a form of identification. Many outlaw motorcycle gang members, other gang members in prison, and some proud military units and fighting battalions have adorned themselves with tattoos: the ominous "Death Before Dishonor" has been popular with young men in the U.S. Marine Corps, and "Harley-Davidson" and "Born to Raise Hell" are typically outlaw biker tattoos.

Clearly, police have an advantage if they can understand and keep abreast of the meaning of skin-art or skin-mutilation, including body piercing. In that way, persons bearing harmless and nonthreatening tattoos can better be sorted out from those whose tattoos convey a more sinister and dangerous meaning.

Survival Skills

As was true of the knowledge needed by police officers, the skills officers need to function effectively in contemporary society have grown significantly in recent decades and have taken some interesting turns. Typing, a skill important in 1951, evolved into needed word processing and other computer skills. The skills of handling police weapons and using them accurately are still needed, as they were in 1951. However, today's weapons skills require critical thinking skills as well, because, thanks to the 1985 *Tennessee vs. Garner* U.S. Supreme Court decision, officers can no longer shoot at fleeing felons who pose no danger to people. Having the skill to shoot accurately, while essential, is now seen within the context of making rapid, data-based discretionary decisions as to the level of force appropriate to specific situations. Such decisions require not only knowledge of police policy and regulations, but the ability to accurately assess a situation and decide quickly on the most appropriate course of action.

For the same reasons that officers must learn to shoot accurately and understand the department's gun-use guidelines, officers must know how to drive defensively, and know the department's guidelines about whether or not to engage in high speed pursuit, or when to disengage, if in a pursuit. These are skills and knowledge which will impact on officer safety, too, as well as the safety of the public.

Officers also need to receive training in alternative driving and car-stop techniques, so they will not be vulnerable to being trapped in their patrol cars when opportunistic criminals stage a crash and activate the safety airbags, pinning police.

OFFICER FIELD SURVIVAL. An officer is cruising down a deserted street in a plainly marked police cruiser in a large city. Suddenly, shots ring out, targeting the car. What does the officer do?

Normal human behavior and police procedures are comfortably congruent when this happens: an officer should get out of the line of fire, pronto! Then the officer must quickly assess the situation, determining the number of assailants and their location, insofar as this can be done. This information must be radioed at once to headquarters, together with a request for immediate assistance. Many departments provide no written guidelines for an event like this, although such an incident is usually covered during the officer's initial training.

Some departments have simulated these exact conditions during training, and have developed a checklist as well as field procedures officers may draw on. The fact that such incidents occur infrequently does not justify failure to prepare personnel for such an ugly eventuality. When an officer's life is on the line, administrative difficulties and field probabilities should not enter the picture. An officer under fire must react instinctively and take evasive measures which can result from training. Any reaction, other than a virtually instinctive one, may mean another dead cop.

There are some specific skills which have been identified for these circumstances. One seeks to minimize police exposure to assaults, and, if there is an assault, prepare officers to defend themselves. Firing positions that decrease the amount of exposed body bulk, while maintaining the ability to return fire, are taught; protective seating positions in a car are shown; and procedures which are reactionary to ambushes are also part of the instruction.

These ideas are not new; they are part of an impressive compilation of existing police defensive tactics drawn together and presented logically as a skill training module. Effective training requires demonstrations and multiple, diverse practice situations. The most important concept in a training module of this sort is this: officers under stress who must make quick, life-saving decisions will revert to techniques ingrained in their earlier training. Hence one's early training, or conditioning, is highly relevant to how an officer will respond to a sudden, life-threatening situation.

PERSUASION—THE SPOKEN WORD. The best police "come-along" is the spoken word! There is none more effective, and there never will be. Hence, police must be afforded as much training in the art of persuasion as a department's curriculum will allow.

Police work is infinitely more difficult without effective verbal and nonverbal communication skills. Often, police have to persuade a resistant individual or group to perform some action that they have refused to do. Effective persuasion techniques can bring about dramatic successes when commands are delivered articulately and with authority. Few professions find the need to rely on persuasion more often, or in more important circumstances, than do officers in the police service.

It's not so much the message itself, as how that message is conveyed, that moves people either positively or negatively. Considerations include both verbal and nonverbal communication skills, such as word usage, voice strength and tone, timing, inflection, posture, eye contact, and other aspects of body language. All these factors bear heavily on whether or not the message is successfully conveyed, as does the setting in which it is delivered.

Whatever means an officer uses to resolve a problem, he or she must act decisively. This is true if the incident is one dealing with drunken or mentally disturbed persons, or persons who are angry and openly hostile. Part of police training must underscore the fact that officers, by their actions and their presence alone, may trigger some people to violent, hostile, or aggressive behavior. Consequently, the words chosen and the physical demeanor an officer displays in addressing a person can be critical in determining the direction a police-citizen contact may take. The *FBI Law Enforcement Bulletin* noted that, for an officer's own protection, he or she should become familiar with, and avoid, antagonistic words and types of overt conduct or body language that might push an individual towards violence:

> ... The police officer must carefully maintain his instrument–speech. He should strive to be as precise with the word as a surgeon is with the scalpel since his operations can also be serious and delicate.

Even the simple utterance, "You're under arrest," might touch off a sudden burst of violence in a suspect. Officers must be aware of such a possibility and train and retrain to learn how to avoid making an inflammatory situation even worse.

Each law enforcement officer should clearly realize the variety of ways in which he or she may appear to others. His or her presence in uniform is a symbol of authority. To many people, this is comforting. To others, it provokes anxiety and fear. This gamut of emotions and uncertainty can spell danger.

Training in the art of persuasion, often professionally referred to by police as "verbal judo," should be taught to a greater extent than it is. Techniques of persuasion could readily be worked into that portion of training which deals with the mechanics of arrest. Persuasion, a frequently underemphasized and underestimated skill, could prove a lifesaver at some time during an officer's career.

Persuasion is only one of many tools, tactics, and techniques available to officers in the performance of their duties. Not every tool, tactic, and technique will be used in every incident. Sometimes one will work, sometimes another is more effective, but usually a combination of several skills will be required. In any event, an understanding of persuasion can help an officer take the upper hand and keep a violent situation from escalating. A three video set, called "Verbal Judo: The Martial Art of Mind and Mouth," has been produced by George J. Thompson. He is the one who originated the phrase "verbal judo," and has also written a book on the subject, *Verbal Judo–The Gentle Art of Persuasion.*

PERSONAL DEFENSE SKILLS. Another essential tool for the working police officer is personal defense training, along with a clear understanding of the force continuum. By knowing the department's policies on acceptable force, it is easier for an officer to stay one step ahead of the aggressive or violent perpetrator. Moreover, officers must be trained, and regularly retrained, in unarmed personal defense, including, but not limited to, baton or PR 24 exercises and hand-to-hand self-defense. There are many effective courses, videos, and books detailing such training. A few videotapes, which are good sellers, include: "Police Control and Restraining Techniques;" "Dynamic Striking Techniques;" and "Surviving Ground Assaults."

A critical element, often overlooked or underemphasized when training officers, is teaching officers to defend themselves while working in teams of two, three, or more. Accordingly, training in defense should not only include basic holds, maneuvers and blows, but new officers should learn to work as part of a team in order to overcome attacks. Training scenarios should feature two officers vs. three perpetrators, two-on-two encounters, and so forth, to prove practical. Officers should be trained in lifelike surroundings, such as buildings or rooms with furniture, stairs, and other obstacles. Clutter-free gymnasium facilities, with padded mats to fall upon, don't cut it any more.

Survival Attitudes

As important as knowledge and skills are in preventing police fatalities, the most important tools in this effort are the attitudes of the officers themselves. By far the most critical training goal is reducing officer fatalities resulting from carelessness and complacency. It has been shown that, when these dangerous mental attitudes are minimized through training and periodic retraining, casualties can be reduced.

OVERCOMING OFFICER CARELESSNESS AND COMPLACENCY. Since the beginning of modern civilization, police have fought criminals. But today, more than ever, police must fight their own carelessness, by far the most common contributor to death among law enforcement officers. Even an effective training program can be rendered ineffective if an officer has a lackadaisical and complacent attitude. It is this state of mind that leads to officer vulnerability and victimization.

Carelessness is often defined as "human error." Though human error can occur in any situation and all occupations, in few professions does it have the potential for deadly risk found in police work. A departure from time-tested patrol procedures can lead to the death of an officer. Of all the officers murdered in the line of duty, research reveals that one of every two was the principal contributor to his or her own death, by not carefully following procedures.

The term human error has a negative connotation, as it denotes ineptness and lack of ability. Carelessness is central to human error. Natural ability, or intense instruction and training, will never completely negate the prospect of human error. But, researchers have discovered that human error is significantly reduced when resources are invested in education and training. Furthermore, continuing in-service training, for street-wise officers, helps reinforce lessons and habits learned earlier, even concepts taught back in recruit school. The point is this: if a police officer is to be made less vulnerable to assault, he or she must be trained, and regularly retrained, so the chance for human error becomes minimal. Carelessness must be trained out of personnel, insofar as that is possible.

A heads-up attitude is the key to combatting carelessness. An officer's attitude is one side of what experts refer to as the "survival triangle," the other two sides being tactics and shooting skills. Certain calls may become routine in the officer's mind, such as the typical domestic dispute that erupts into noisy fighting and culminates with police intervention. Such family disturbances are ordinarily not too hard to resolve, once police get the principals calmed down and separated, perhaps taking one into custody. Although such an outcome is the norm, data show that the domestic dispute is one of the most dangerous police calls. Further, research shows that in many cases where there were police fatalities, the officers anticipated routine and uneventful calls. The importance of an alert attitude must be drummed into police officers, because complacency can surely lead to serious injury or death.

Carelessness also frequently characterizes the police response to burglary alarms, because about 95 of every 100 such events prove to be false alarms. It is the ones that prove "hot" that do the careless officers in. Staying heads-up for every response is urgent, and also the challenge to police.

While the mortality rate is way too high, by no means is the murder of every police officer a product of carelessness. In some instances, an unprovoked sudden attack or a sniper's bullet can end the life of a top notch officer. Casualties of this nature are unavoidable. Ironically, some officers murdered in the line of duty were lulled into complacency by the repetitive nature of the job, like the burglar alarm call described above, even though they were certainly aware of the constant dangers involved. Typically, in such incidents, the officer's misjudgment was contributory to his or her own murder. Misjudgments and carelessness, in patrol work, are often brought on by the numbing predictability of the daily grind.

Complacency plagues even the most competent officers, at one time or another, during their careers. Real-life patrol bears little resemblance to television where several catastrophic incidents an officer may never face in a career happen one after the other, in a one-hour episode. The action found on real patrol duty does not provide the second-by-second excitement required to fuel a Hollywood shoot-em-up. Actually, officers spend most of their time engaged in unexciting, noncrime fighting activities.

The complacency syndrome has not escaped comment by experts. For example, former FBI Director Clarence M. Kelley observed:

> Complacency is always a dangerous foe. For a law enforcement officer, it can be a deadly enemy.
>
> ....[An officer] must constantly remind himself that there is nothing routine in law enforcement duty. He cannot shirk that duty even when it—as it frequently does—propels him suddenly and without warning into the jaws of grave human conflict. At these dangerous times, an officer's only companion is his alertness... It is likely that there will always be ambush assassins, frenzied terrorists, ruthless killers, desperate felons, and emotionally overwrought persons to threaten the lives of law enforcement officers. Our complacency, however, must never be permitted to aid this perilous band of police killers.

Kelley's message is clear: officers must be constantly alert to danger. But being alert is more than just being aware to the potential danger of a situation: it encompasses the officers' insight into how they will be perceived by the public, what their role is in a police interaction, and how well they can adapt to those circumstances and variables.

Former Director Kelley is not the only FBI leader to see complacency as a condition which paves the road to disaster. Earlier, the Bureau's legendary Director, J. Edgar Hoover, wrote that:

> The tragic total of policemen slain last year brings out crucial points that all officers should remember: (1) complacency is most dangerous, and (2) there is no such thing as a "routine" arrest.

Few people, including veteran law enforcement officers, take kindly to being forever told what they must do. For that reason, it is best to lay the foundation for an alert and "heads-up" attitude in early recruit training. Newly hired police cadets are eager to learn, and if the lessons are presented in a relevant way, the information will be remembered over many, many years of service.

A slogan that needs to be drummed into police recruits, is "360 degrees around you." This phrase reminds them to watch their backs and focus on every aspect of the crime scene. The person hunkered down behind a car, across the street from the bank, might be the lookout with a shotgun. Not surprisingly, carelessness, stemming from overconfidence and responding to too many routine cases, usually increases with experience and longevity in the profession. Therefore, regular in-service refresher sessions for all police officers are essential. Such on-going instruction should reemphasize the fundamental safety principles taught during recruit training.

Another important survival consideration calls for officers on routine patrol to be ever alert to whomever may be encountered in certain places, and appreciate the mental stresses which may be nagging people at specific locales. For example, officers should know the location of residences for abused and battered spouses and children. Should there be reports of disturbances there, or men are seen lurking nearby, responding officers may anticipate encountering people under immense psychological stress who may react aggressively to authority with little or no provocation. In fact, attacks without warning may be more likely in this setting than in many others.

PIERCE BROOKS' LIST OF DANGERS. Pierce R. Brooks, homicide detective in Joseph Wambaugh's nonfiction best-seller, *The Onion Field*, devised an impressive list of dangers to police as relates to field survival. It is important to realize that these elements are based more on attitudes than skills. He included the list in his classic officer survival book, "*...Officer Down, Code Three.*" The list, set out below, is very cogent as it identifies officers' bad practices which may lead them to becoming victims:

1. Bad attitude
2. Sleepy or asleep on duty

3. Taking a bad position
4. Missing the danger signs
5. Failure to watch hands
6. Poor or no search
7. Relaxing too soon
8. Improper use of handcuffs
9. Poor care and use of weapons
10. Tombstone courage

Brooks' list stems from his earlier experience as a member of the Los Angeles Police Department's special investigations team. Comprised of experienced investigators, this team is responsible for reconstructing all officer-involved shootings in the city which resulted in the injury or death of any person. The resources and numerical strength of the Los Angeles Police Department justify the presence of such a special after action investigation team, just as such a team may be feasible for all but the smallest departments to have. Smaller departments may make arrangements to call upon a larger force to help on an "as needed" basis to reconstruct an incident.

The importance of developing an officer survival program based on local circumstances, as suggested in Brooks' book, cannot be over-emphasized. Therefore, whenever there is a serious attack on an officer, even if it did not prove fatal, not only a thorough investigation, but a complete analysis should be made. Both may prove of extraordinary value in drawing up subsequent training simulations, revising field procedures and, hopefully, in preventing future officer victims. Conventional wisdom and common sense is, that when behavior such as portrayed in Brooks' list can be neutralized through training and supervision, casualties can be reduced. Of course, training needs to be based on more than conventional wisdom and common sense.

Effective Training Strategies

While the importance of training for law enforcement personnel has been widely recognized, it is important to realize that not all training programs are equally effective in preparing officers to avoid becoming fatalities. Educational research which has emerged over the past two decades provides evidence as to the kind of teaching most effective in producing higher student achievement. The findings of this research need to be understood by those responsible for planning training programs for police officers. Among the elements of effective teaching that have been repeatedly demonstrated in this body of research are the following:

1. **Clear instructional focus.** A preplanned curriculum which clearly specifies intended outcomes is a critical element in assuring that officers learn the knowledge, develop the attitudes, and refine the skills of the profession. Intended outcomes are sometimes expressed in the form of goals and objectives, but whatever the form, the more instructors and trainees share a common understanding of the purposes for the training and the intended results, the more likely the training is to be effective.

2. **High expectations.** Communicating to recruits the high expectations held for them, by not only their supervisors but by the public, helps ensure that they will put forth their best efforts. Research has shown that teachers have different levels of expectation for various students, that they often unintentionally convey lower levels of expectations for certain students, and that these expectations have a significant impact on student achievement. Unfortunately, it has frequently been students who come from lower income families or minority groups for whom teachers demonstrate lower expectations. However, when instructors learn what specific behaviors subtly communicate high expectations, learning opportunities in the classroom can be dramatically enhanced.

More than a dozen specific teacher behaviors have been identified that convey high expectations to students. For instance, students sense that teachers expect more from them when they are called on to speak more often, when they are asked more probing questions, when specific elements of a strong performance are pointed out, and when the teacher interacts informally with them during breaks. While remembering which recruit's family just welcomed a new baby, or which ones particularly enjoy hunting or fishing, may seem irrelevant to the training process, expressing such information during informal contacts has been far more frequent with students for whom the teacher has high expectations. The message is that the instructor values them—the students—as worthwhile, interesting people. Effort to distribute participation opportunities and personal contacts equitably can result in higher achievement, especially among those whom the instructor may consider less capable.

3. **Time on task.** The allocation of time during a training program needs to reflect priority outcomes. Not surprisingly, research has

demonstrated that students learn more when more instructional time is devoted to an objective. One has reason to question the priorities of a program which allocates 30 hours to training in word processing, but only three hours to training in verbal persuasion, or only five hours to field survival.

4. **Engaged time.** Not only is the total amount of time allocated to various training objectives significant, but the extent to which training strategies engage the attention of students is also critical. Passive listening is rarely as impactful as activities which consistently engage students. Active learning strategies may be as simple as pausing during a lecture to give students a question to consider in pairs, or in small groups, before sharing responses with the whole class. This provides a far higher degree of engagement than traditional questioning during a lecture when only one student may be actively engaged and the rest passively listen.

Recognizing that today's trainees have grown up in a television generation, the use of materials which provide realistic sights and sounds, such as in a video, is important to holding the students' attention. Because television watching is a passive pursuit, planning small group interaction with large group sharing about the program's content is critical if students are to be mentally engaged. Simulations or role plays which require students to act and react as if they were in life-threatening situations can ensure even greater engagement. Realistic settings for simulations, such as convenience stores or rooms in a home, add to their impact. Interactive video simulations using computer-based technology can provide the highest level of engagement as students individually respond to situations and are given feedback as to their level of performance.

5. **Frequent monitoring with feedback and reinforcement.** High tech simulations are not the only aspect of training where feedback is important. Research on effective teaching shows that students learn more when their performance is monitored frequently and they are given specific feedback and reinforcement. As part of the clear instructional focus, both trainers and recruits need to know what the standards for performance are and receive ongoing information as to their progress toward meeting the standards.

The elements of effective teaching just described are currently evident in some police academies and other law enforcement training programs. Those responsible for training are encouraged to consider these elements as they plan. The instructional focus needed to prevent police fatalities has been outlined earlier in this chapter as we considered the knowledge, skills, and attitudes officers need to survive.

Traditional classroom instructional methods remain a staple of police training. While classroom lectures are suitable for teaching law, sociology, and other passive subjects, their effectiveness is increased when instructors plan for active involvement of students during the class session. In addition to traditional lectures, newer instructional strategies and resources which can be useful in training sessions illustrate the enormous potential for improving training effectiveness.

Enhancing Engagement

The importance of preparing officers to work in teams of two, three, or more was pointed out earlier in our discussion of personal defense skills. Implementing training strategies in which small groups of recruits are assigned to deliberate over dilemmas provided by the instructor not only engages the students' attention, but helps prepare them for working together.

Use of videotapes in training, with appropriate relevant discussion, also increases engagement. It is not uncommon for recruits to study real life videos, recorded at violent crime scenes by cameras in patrol cars, security surveillance cameras, or tapes from accidental bystanders who happened to have video cameras, as in the Rodney King incident. The instructor will start and stop the video, calling attention to critical junctures, and then discuss these and safety procedures with the cadets. Students will be tested on recall and perception, making sure that they are aware of all the dangers present. Some trainers will even show sequences from "Cops," or other television shows, and ask officers how they would have handled the volatile situations portrayed on the screen.

Closed circuit law enforcement television networks are another means by which officers may be engaged and very actively learn. The value of these delivery systems, particularly for officers in small, rural forces, cannot be overstated. Closed circuit television should be a staple in every training center.

Companies, directing their efforts at presenting quality and realistic training for police, have produced video clips of various complicated and stressful situations. Some forces still use training films, but film is rapidly being replaced by more modern video technology. The action-scenes show the explosive potential of numerous interactions, and set out the appropriate police responses. Trainees can learn by seeing dozens of probable scenarios, instead of merely being lectured about them. Lessons taught by books, and the experiences recounted by seasoned officers and trainees, will be reinforced by the use of action training videos. The value of continued and memorable visual and vicarious reinforcement in police education is very important to modern police officer training.

A time-tested training tool, originally put out years ago on film, is titled "Deadly Force Decisions," directed by Dennis Anderson. The two part video, which comes with an instructor's manual, slides, and sample tests, puts officers in situations where, in a split second, they have to decide whether or not to fire on a suspect who confronts them from the screen. Another standard video, also directed by Dennis Anderson, is "Surviving Edged Weapons." It covers the proper way to defend against knives, their killing distances, and how to justify one's defensive tactics in court.

"Street Survival" is a popular workshop, presented by Calibre Press, utilizing video, notebooks, and personal instruction. It is presented in major cities throughout the United States on a frequent basis and occasionally in Canada. Calibre Press has also published three books: *Street Survival, The Tactical Edge,* and *Tactics for Criminal Patrol.* These landmark publications, written by Charles Remsberg, are remarkable adjuncts to the workshop.

There are several other training organizations which have programs and publications which address officer safety. These include the American Society of Law Enforcement Trainers, the Institute of Police Technology and Management, and the International Association of Law Enforcement Firearms Instructors.

Realistic training media remind officers that they must always be alert, disciplined, and ready to make immediate decisions in matters of fatal force. Meanwhile, the public demands that police officers remain sensitive as to the consequences of life and death split-second decisions which might be forced upon them.

Simulations

The value of simulation training as an instructional strategy is immense. For example, officers find themselves in some of the most congested, cluttered locations imaginable as they go about their work. Such places as kitchens, living or family rooms, restaurants, bars, and pool halls are not necessarily the most orderly places, especially if the occupants or proprietors put no priority on orderliness. Add to the clutter the fact that when there is an attack with a gun, it is highly likely to come at a distance of no more than five feet. Knife and other non-firearm attacks usually occur in close quarters, too, though rock and bottle tossing incidents are notable exceptions, The scene of an attack, especially when police respond to a domestic quarrel, will usually be cluttered with household furnishings, while outdoor attacks likely will occur in parking lots, alleys full of trash and perhaps abandoned autos, or sidewalks with shrubs, trees, and other obstructions or hiding places. If assaulted while transporting a suspect in the car, an officer may be pinned against the steering wheel.

Therefore, it makes sense for trainers to create authentic mock scenes. In simulated settings, the student faces a realistic situation, instead of the one-dimensional experience of learning in a sterile gymnasium. A resourceful trainer may secure permission to train in such places as convenience stores, banks, commercial parking lots, schools, or some other business locales to provide settings for simulated police encounters.

Not all mock scenes portray violence. Actors, coached by the instructors, will role-play the parts of perpetrators or innocent bystanders. The trainees will receive a description of the suspect, get in a patrol car, and respond exactly as they would in a real emergency. The scene is interactive in that the "criminals" will tailor their actions to those of the cop. If the officer makes a mistake, the perpetrator, or an accomplice, will take full advantage of the oversight. The mock-scenes are graded, with live monitors watching the whole situation unfold. Ordinarily, recruits have to successfully pass a certain percentage of mock-scenes, or they won't graduate.

For additional realism, some instructors supplement the action by providing the armed officers and criminals with paintball bullets. Brawls, traffic stops, and citizen encounters can take place at outside settings, with family calls and other disturbances simulated in buildings or in home-like settings.

Those departments that are equipped to provide trainees with videotaped instant replays of simulated encounters can enhance the training. Immediately playing back a video can make dangerous practices and procedural errors obvious. As the class watches itself on the screen, sometimes with understandable amusement, trainees see firsthand the importance of proper and safe police work. Whatever entertainment or humor is evident can make the scene even more memorable. State-of-the art technology captures the attention of the trainee so completely that the lessons learned are more likely to be retained for a career.

High-Tech Simulations

Another training strategy is to set up three-dimensional reactive targets. These targets are made of urethane, can survive up to 2,500 rounds, and are easily patched. Both male and female models look human, and accessories such as badges, knives and automatic weapons can be purchased to make the models resemble good or bad guys. These models make it necessary for an officer in training to determine instantly whether or not to shoot at the subject. When set up in a realistic fashion, hidden behind trees or in buildings, these targets allow trainees to fire real bullets, and subjects go down, with good shot placement. These reactive targets make training remarkably authentic.

One of the most widely-used training courses today, popular in both the United States and Canada, is called F.A.T.S., or firearms training simulation. The program utilizes big screen video controlled by a computer and an operator. A student officer, armed with an electronically interactive pistol, responds to many very deadly situations that are realistically displayed on the screen. The computer operator can control the actions on the big screen: he or she could cause the shooter's hands to come up in surrender, cause him to fire on the officer, or he could even make the shooter go down wounded and come back up again, shooting, although this scenario will not happen if the trainee fires a lethal shot. All in all, how the suspect will react is largely dependent on the trainee's shooting and the way in which he or she responds to the overall situation. The setting, also, includes a few common pieces of furniture or props for the officer to use as cover.

When the scene is over, the trainee is graded on voice utilization and authority, use of cover, marksmanship, and general procedure.

During the critique, the trainer/operator will make red dots appear over the on screen suspects, so the accuracy of the officer's shooting can be judged.

Many large forces and police academies have F.A.T.S. permanently set up, often in a trailer. Meanwhile, of benefit to smaller departments, are training companies that will bring a portable unit to their area. This sophisticated system can be customized for specialist officers as well. For example, it is frequently used in conjunction with training officer-dog teams where the twosome is expected to respond appropriately to a variety of simulations programmed into the F.A.T.S.

A critique should be held at the end of every training session, with both the staff and the participants offering constructive criticism. During such critiques, instructors should thoughtfully answer questions raised by officers.

Use of interactive video and computer-based simulations has dramatically improved the degree of realism in the situations trainees face, even simulating the stress of actual emergency situations. Computer simulations are effective training for far more than hand-eye coordination, in that complex situations are presented in which students must make life or death decisions in split second time frames.

Training to Improve the Odds

While all of the training strategies described here can improve the odds for preventing officer fatality, it is important to keep in mind the kinds of situations in which officers are most likely to become complacent, thereby putting themselves in jeopardy. For example, officers frequently underestimate the danger implicit in a stress call, such as a domestic violence or other disturbance reports. From 1960 through 1994, 474 officers were murdered while responding to these kinds of calls, a very significant 16.6 percent of the 2,626 U.S. police officers murdered over that time span. Interactive videos, actual crime footage, professional books, and mock scenes which are videotaped and analyzed, help remind law enforcement personnel of the sudden unexpected twists and imminent dangers which can emerge when responding to high risk calls. Always being aware of the danger can only lead to a more attentive attitude and reduce the probability that an officer will fall prey to carelessness.

Summary

Police officer training is like good sex: you can never get enough of it, and what you do get should be of high quality, and enticingly presented!

Chapter 6

GETTING THE HOUSE IN ORDER

Meaningful casualty reduction is much more than pursuing highly visible, trendy measures, such as survival training, purchasing twenty first century hardware, or practicing SWAT operations. Rather, more attention must be afforded to the mundane, but important matters, which the administration can put in place to assure that officers operate in a safe environment.

What the Brass Must Do

The everyday management decisions of a force fall to the ranking personnel, known as The Brass. Whether that title is one of affection or derision, these are the administrators responsible for implementing programs and establishing policies for the entire force, some of which have major impact on the safety of police officers. Often, these decisions are more important than the troops appreciate, or are willing to admit.

Ranking personnel must be certain that procedures manuals are up to-date, and that supervision is provided throughout the force, irrespective of the time of day, or the location. The Brass should recognize the significance of first-level supervisors, and conscientiously support these persons who have the toughest job on the force, while holding them to a high standard of performance. Top administrators need to set out realistic guidelines governing off-shift jobs for police, to protect officers from over extending themselves or overdoing their physical limits. The administration may, also, consider the appropriateness of implementing an auxiliary, or reserve, police officer program, and set out incentives to assure that officers maintain a high level of physical fitness.

Procedures Manuals

Adequate, up-to-date, utilitarian procedures manuals are essential to help officers clearly understand their duties and responsibilities. The written guidelines should be simple, technically concise, complete, drafted in positive, rather than negative language, and divided by topic into sections, with an index. Police administrators should prepare and make available detailed procedural guidelines covering about every anticipated circumstance which may be expected within a force's jurisdiction. For example, adhering to national guidelines or state training curricula may apply to most incidents, but guidelines should be drafted to cover dangerous situations that are commonplace and specific to an area. Of course, procedures manuals need regular updating and should be enlarged upon as circumstances change or new conditions present themselves.

A department needs to regularly adapt important sections of its procedures manual into training bulletins and review them at roll call sessions. This type of a bulletin contains a synthesis of many, many pages from the procedural manual and is exactly the type of training aid that helps an officer, almost intuitively, confront risky circumstances with a minimum of danger. If police are unfamiliar with or unable to recall specific procedures and training information, incidents may unnecessarily escalate into violence.

The International Association of Chiefs of Police established the National Law Enforcement Policy Center in 1987, as a result of a cooperative agreement with the U.S. Justice Department's Bureau of Justice Assistance. The Center has assisted police agencies across the nation with the critical, yet difficult, task of developing and refining law enforcement policies and police procedures. The topics addressed by the Center include some of the most difficult issues facing law enforcement administrators. Departments of all sizes will find the Policy Center to be a valuable resource as they go about drafting or updating policies and procedures manuals to reflect national standards.

Effective Supervision

Constructive supervision and positive discipline are essential ingredients if training programs and new, innovative approaches to patrol work are to be safe and effective. Take, for instance, an officer's bad habits, like those identified by Pierce Brooks in Chapter 5. If they go uncorrected, they become ingrained, destroying any benefits from otherwise effective training.

Discipline is even more essential in police work than it is in most other endeavors. However, police personnel typically share a common bond and are a closely-knit group, a team, similar to military personnel. Mutual feelings and comradeship are beneficial, but may also wreak havoc with the disciplinary system. No team player likes to criticize or see a fellow officer reprimanded for mishandling a boring, tedious aspect of patrol, especially if he or she would have done the same thing under similar circumstances.

The solution to this complex aspect of interpersonal relations rests with the supervisor, who first must detect a problem. Once aware of the situation, be it an infraction, a bad habit, or another problem, the supervisor must react to it appropriately and constructively. But, the supervisor must not permit a sense of empathy to influence his or her supervisory responsibilities. Looking the other way, when confronted by a disciplinary issue would foster carelessness and complacency, the two greatest dangers to police.

Let's frankly recognize the most important member of any police force: the first level supervisor! These representatives present officer concerns to management, and relay management positions (sometimes a seemingly endless number of administrative fiats) back to officers. These are the persons who end up in the middle of whatever is happening! First level supervisors must be very capable if they are to work effectively.

Every officer's safety is related to having an adequate number of qualified and dedicated first level field supervisors, called sergeants in most departments. If first level supervisors are careless, sloppy, unmotivated, or act as if they are just "promoted police officers," the vitality of the force will suffer, as will discipline, direction, and control. Having poor quality first level supervisors almost always guarantees that officers will not perform their work in accordance with procedures, policies, and guidelines. Conversely, respected, motivated and perceptive first level supervisors, who have their fingers on the pulse of the organization, assume dynamic leadership roles by insisting upon safe and positive performance from subordinate personnel. First level supervisors, working at full potential, can bring a level of excellence to a force that is stunning.

The Officer with Two Jobs

Moonlighting has been discouraged by managers in almost all professions. The usual criticism holds that a person can't work two jobs and contribute his or her best efforts to either. In police work, moonlighting is also frowned upon, or prohibited, because it may contribute to an overworked officer being inattentive. While all of these criticisms may be valid, most officers moonlight out of necessity to supplement modest police salaries. The issue of pay inequities begs for a solution.

In the meantime, an officer who has worked another job before reporting to duty, can be expected to show signs of weariness, functioning below maximum efficiency and, those who are slated to moonlight after their police shift may feel under pressure to physically save themselves. Cops "taking it easy" can endanger the safety of their associates. Alertness, the hallmark of police efficiency and survival, will suffer.

The debilitating effects of moonlighting prompted the late FBI Director J. Edgar Hoover to stridently deplore moonlighting:

> Law enforcement is highly exacting work. It demands mental and physical alertness, single-mindedness, dedication, and enthusiasm for effective performance. To fully discharge his responsibilities and do a creditable job, an officer should devote all his energy to his enforcement duties. Unfortunately, many cannot do this. They are required to "moonlight" in order to give their families a decent standard of living.

Director Hoover closed by declaring that: "All communities should pay policemen suitable wages and let moonlighting pass from the scene."

Controlling moonlighting is easier said than done. Many forces have tried to limit an officer's moonlighting to no more than four hours each day, and preferably less. They argue that an officer working more than four hours cannot possibly be mentally prepared to hit the street in peak physical or mental condition. Other departments have restricted moonlighting to a maximum of 20 hours a week, and some have banned certain types of work. Most forces have policies that require officers to secure written approval before being allowed to work off duty.

The moonlighting issue nags at law enforcement agencies and officers alike. There is no easy solution. But steps should be taken by each department, where moonlighting continues to be a problem, to correct pay inequities or to find ways to limit the number of off-shift hours worked. Whatever action is taken, one fact is certain: the extra income will be meaningless if the second job induces a weakness in an officer that leads to his or her gross negligence while on duty.

Often obscured in any discussion of moonlighting is the double standard fostered by some departments: requests by the administration that officers work double shifts. If a force fails to monitor which officers are working well beyond their normal hours, it places employees at risk, just as if the personnel were holding down second jobs. This is a pervasive internal problem and, despite the dangers, it often goes ignored.

Auxiliary Police

Many forces have a part-time, trained auxiliary police unit to relieve regular officers from time-consuming, mundane, noncrime fighting activities. An auxiliary force, properly trained and equipped, and knowledgeable of police methods, can lighten the work load and enhance the safety of regular personnel.

There is a growing and impressive precedent for volunteer auxiliary police units. Some of the largest forces have thousands of trained auxiliary police who are uniformed, but in a manner distinctly different from the regular police. They are equipped with handcuffs, nightsticks, and walkie-talkies, but most do not bear firearms. Their primary mission is not to apprehend criminals, but to assist the public with routine matters and to watch out for and report suspicious activity. The auxiliaries, in essence, are trained eyes and ears, alert to the warning signs of potential trouble. When regular police respond to a suspicious circumstance, reported by auxiliaries, they are more likely to arrive on the scene forewarned of unusual or potentially ugly conditions.

A host of departments have added still another group of enthusiastic volunteers to help out at headquarters, in clerical and support roles. This is a body of trained senior citizens, whose efforts have helped cut down on the workload of regular police employees. These senior volunteers save money in a department's budget and enhance officer safety. Furthermore, the community service gives them an interesting and productive pursuit for their golden years. Some other forces have found that explorer scout troops may perform with distinction in a similar fashion.

Freeing regular police from mundane activities, which might lull an officer into vulnerability at a critical time, is helpful. So is having a force of alert eyes and ears on the street. There are many virtues to implementing auxiliary police, and senior or explorer scout programs, in forces which do not have them.

Physical Fitness Programs

Many police personnel eat the wrong food, are overweight, smoke too much, drink too much coffee or alcohol, and don't get enough exercise. Occupational hazards? Hardly, since these conditions need not be, for each officer has control over whether or not to smoke, what to eat and drink, as well as exercise practices. It is simply that many people lack the personal discipline and the willpower to translate one's resolve into action.

Officers, who are not in good physical condition, endanger not only their own lives, but those of other police. Not surprisingly, out-of-shape cops lose some of their physical and mental keenness in crisis situations. And it is well known that police work and crisis management are integrally related to one another.

Persons in less than top physical condition are more subject to on the-job injuries. They are also more likely to suffer from heart attacks, high blood pressure, circulatory diseases, and back problems.

Not many police forces have implemented mandatory physical fitness training or weight maintenance programs. Moreover, very few forces have offered a reward or incentive program for officers who keep themselves trim and fit. It is worthy of note that of those departments experimenting with rewards or incentives for fitness, the programs have been popular and a morale booster for employees. Interestingly, research discloses that prison inmates, as a group, are in better physical condition than police and have greater endurance! This is insulting, as well as alarming, and police officers and administrators should be challenged to redress it.

Good physical fitness is good personal business. Athletes know, and police should, too, that staying free from injury begins with proper exercise and conditioning. Departments should insist upon fitness for all personnel.

Sharpening Field Operations

Operations constitute the fieldwork of a police department and should produce maximum efficiency with the least expense and effort. Operations, performed by uniformed and detective personnel, are directed toward achieving a specific purpose. In law enforcement these are services rendered to the public—patrol, traffic regulation, and crime prevention and investigation.

Uniformed officers perform almost all of the basic police tasks and services. A police force, therefore, is really no better than its uniformed personnel, including its first level supervisors. The existence of an alert, adequately equipped, well-supervised and properly trained patrol force is the best deterrent to criminal activity. Citizens judge the police, and extend or withhold their support and cooperation, on the basis of the appearance, attitude, and conduct of the personnel in uniform. So an effective program depends to a great extent upon the ability of a force to execute basic police procedures. The safety of personnel is related to effective field procedures as well.

As we move toward the millennium, several forces have made some changes in their traditional police field procedures. These departments have devised a variety of directed patrol programs, placing uniformed personnel in more of a proactive, rather than reactive, mode. Innovations include such strategies as community policing, integrated criminal apprehension programs, and split force patrols. These programs try to involve the community in systematically targeting crime and other negative conditions which warrant greater-than-usual police coverage and time.

By no means should the newer strategies lead administrators or officers into complacency, for danger still awaits the personnel responsible for carrying out these programs. While modern approaches may differ from the more traditional ones, the same old risks apply and officers will continue to become casualties.

Offering Variety on Patrol

Police patrol work, the mainstay of law enforcement globally, is often unpleasant and boring, without much humor. Yet, there are some occasions when police are able to express sympathy and give succor to people, which can be gratifying. Although people are not often aggressive towards police, neither are they usually positive and affectionate, either.

There are some important changes taking place in police patrol. One new strategy is community-oriented police and problem solving, COPPS for short. Community policing stems from earlier experiments with team policing and other initiatives. This approach is characterized by a high level of direct contact with people in neighborhoods. The concept strives to reunite police with the community, by encouraging uniformed officers to become more sensitive to community needs. Personnel involved in community policing attempt to achieve order through a working partnership with families, schools, and neighborhood and merchant associations. In effect, its aim is to get police back on the beat, breaking the historic union between an officer's seat of the pants and the patrol car seat. It seeks to counter the traditional isolation of police from the community, so common with car patrol officers.

COPPS has gone a long way toward casting uniformed officers as helpful "people," not just faceless entities. The program leads to more interesting and challenging patrol work, but leaves room for a variety of specialized jobs that officers may assume, especially in larger forces. There is always a demand for qualified officers to serve on SWAT or ERT teams, in helicopters, as hostage negotiators, accident investigators, canine handlers, and other important positions.

In contrast to a few decades earlier, there are fresh challenges for officers as they go about their patrols. It is hoped that, with new approaches to patrol and evolving dangers, officer vigilance will rise to the occasion. When an officer knows a job and appreciates the risks involved, he or she is less apt to drift into complacency and, hence, is less likely to be injured on duty.

Handling and Transporting Prisoners

The supervision and transport of prisoners in the field should never be treated as routine. Transporting prisoners presents untold dangers to officers as well as to suspects and the public. In short, no prisoner should ever be left unsupervised until he or she is securely locked in the jail. Even there, most sizeable lockups have a person in charge of monitoring the cells by video camera. And an officer should never walk in front of a prisoner!

The first step, after a prisoner has been taken into custody and is immobilized, is to conduct a thorough search of his or her person and clothing. Less-than-thorough searches have resulted in many police fatalities. In one Oklahoma incident, arresting police conducted a sloppy search of a prisoner who, later, while being transported by auto to jail, murdered the officer driving the car. In their search, officers had initially found several rounds of pistol ammunition in the suspect's pockets. Yet, even though the suspect was searched three separate times by three different officers, and the discovery of small arms ammunition was known to all, the searches failed to uncover a small pistol taped to the suspect's upper right bicep. And, to make the oversight even worse, the suspect had made a slit in his jacket for easy access to the pistol, something that also went undetected.

The only solution, to this kind of fatal error, is better training, designed to regularize and habitualize the pre-transportation search of a prisoner. In the incident described above, "ammunition" should have instinctively meant "gun" to the officers, and the searches should have been pressed with intensity. Additionally, written guidelines outlining searches, methods, and procedures should be produced and made mandatory reading for all officers, both during and after police academy training. A training bulletin, which covers the techniques for apprehending, searching, and transporting suspects, should be published and specify the department's procedures for approaching a suspect, searching him or her (and a vehicle, should there be one), and handcuffing and transporting the prisoner. The bulletin must be painstakingly precise and detailed, spelling out every element necessary to assure proper safety precautions.

While the safest method of transporting prisoners is by paddy wagon, not all forces, especially those with few personnel, have access to a special purpose vehicle. Instead, most officers have to transport prisoners in standard police cars. When that is the case, the precautionary measures outlined in training manuals and academy instruction should be followed scrupulously. This should include handcuffing prisoners with their hands behind the back.

Strange, unexpected, and unanticipated events can occur in cars. In one instance, a deputy sheriff had handcuffed and searched a prisoner, then placed him in the back seat of a patrol car with no safety partition. On the way to jail, the suspect unlatched the back of the driver's seat and suddenly rammed it forward with his feet, pinning the deputy against the steering wheel. The deputy was savagely beaten. In another instance, officers examining a squad car found that sometime earlier prisoners had stuffed hypodermic syringes between the seats to hamper searchers.

With the hands of each prisoner restrained, any attempt to stash contraband or to assault the transporting officer will be extremely awkward, if not impossible. The transporting officer, if he or she did not conduct the initial search, should routinely and carefully, re-search the prisoner. Handcuffs and other restraining devices need to be applied according to prescribed police department procedures. Metallic handcuffs should meet the voluntary national standards set out by the National Institute of Law Enforcement and Criminal Justice. Police training courses and manuals should detail the proper use of such devices. And officers should never be foolish enough to think that a handcuffed prisoner is harmless, because some prisoners are proficient at slipping, shimming, or picking handcuffs.

Department policy may specify the circumstances which require handcuffs, but the final decision is always up to the arresting officer. The decision should be based upon the officer's perception and assessment of the situation, and the necessity to protect himself, the public, and the prisoner. A suspect may appear to be cooperative or docile, but that is no guarantee that there will not later be an attempt to overpower the officer or escape, should an opportunity present itself.

Once a prisoner is in the vehicle and is heading for his moment of truth at the jail, he may unpredictably react with sudden fury. Therefore, an officer should never try to second-guess the prisoner's state of mind and, on that basis, decide against applying restraints. A test of a good officer is his or her ability to "talk" a suspect into wearing handcuffs for the ride to headquarters. If there is ever any question about handcuffing: apply the restraints!

There have been occasions when an officer was shot and killed, after losing control of his own weapon, while transporting a prisoner. This has happened even when the prisoner was handcuffed, though cuffs lessen the prospect. If the suspect cannot be transported in the back seat, seasoned officers routinely move their handgun to the side away from the prisoner. If the officer is driving, for example, and a prisoner is seated to the right, the gun should be kept on the officer's left side. Uncomfortable, perhaps, but the safety margin increases for an officer who takes advantage of this common sense precautionary measure. The gun is out of reach to the suspect but still accessible to the driver.

The Federal Aviation Administration, a branch of the U.S. Department of Transportation, has published regulations which spell out conditions for the transportation of prisoners under the control of armed law enforcement escorts. These are contained in Section 108.21 of Part 108 of the Federal Aviation Regulations which pertain to Airplane Operator Security.

Each commercial carrier has promulgated policy about transporting prisoners. While there are similarities among policies, there are some differences among carriers. But, generally speaking, the airlines require regular tickets be purchased for each person travelling, officers and prisoners alike. Arrangements must be made upon ticketing to list the personnel who will be armed, and each carrier has its own forms to be completed by the escorts. These require that officers specify a "security designation" for each prisoner and detail the arrangements required for each prisoner. Generally, these designations are either maximum or minimum. Since a designation of "maximum" has been known to cause a carrier to deny passage to the prisoner and escorts, officers usually declare that the prisoner is "minimum," so as not to cause unnecessary difficulties.

Carriers usually require the presence of at least one more officer than the total number of prisoners under escort. Understandably, it is customary to board officers and prisoners before boarding the civilian passengers. Upon reaching their destination, law enforcement waits for the passengers to disembark before the police entourage leaves the aircraft.

While there are no hard rules regarding restraints, most carriers prefer the low-key approach of unrestrained prisoners. Accordingly, the carriers will seat the officers and prisoners in the rear-most seats, with the prisoners by the windows, so as to limit contact with other passengers. On wide bodied aircraft, the prisoner is usually sandwiched in the middle section, flanked by officers. While on board, prisoners are usually treated the same as other passengers, offered food and non alcohol drinks, unless the escorting officers specify otherwise.

Experience has shown that, when officers comply with the carriers' policies and are experienced in the care, custody, and transportation of prisoners, the prospect of a regrettable incident is virtually nil.

Police Canine Teams and Officer Safety

It was the winter of 1988 in Prince Rupert, British Columbia, a small and peaceful Canadian town, just 30 miles south of the Alaska wilderness. A dusting of light snow covered the tree branches and the ground. The mountie and his partner were following the fresh footprints on a winding trail leading around the hill. It was an easy track, as tracks go: distinct footprints in the fresh snow that seemed almost too obvious. The Royal Canadian Mounted Police corporal and his partner of eight years were, unbeknown to them, walking straight into a deadly ambush.

The man they were tracking, sought for a senseless act of domestic violence, lay in wait less than 50 yards ahead, on his belly in sniper position, a hunting rifle pressed to his shoulder. Concealed by dense underbrush and rocks, the gunman had an unobstructed view of anyone following the footprints he had intentionally left in the snow.

Suddenly, the mountie's alert partner raised his rugged head, sniffed the air, looked all around and abandoned the trail, abruptly leading the lawman into the thick brush, rocks, and trees. Quietly cresting the hill, the two readily spotted the sniper below, his rifle trained on the path they had been walking moments before.

Cautiously making their way toward the gunman, a twig snapped under the lawman's boot. Startled, the sniper turned the gun toward the noise, but he was much too slow: in but an instant, the trusted partner was on the dismayed would-be assassin, disarming and completely overwhelming him.

Claude Wilcott, 32-years-old and a corporal for less than six months, had just been saved from deadly ambush by his partner, an 85 pound German shepherd dog, named Buck. The corporal is just one more of an uncounted number of police officers worldwide who owe their lives to the alert senses of highly-trained police canines.

A well-trained police service dog, with keen hearing and extraordinary olfactory capabilities, can help keep cops alive. To assure an extra margin of safety for his human partner, a general patrol dog, at the very least, should be able to track reliably in the city and the country; conduct an area search and a building search; and perform criminal apprehension and handler protection, without putting the public at risk. Many police forces go far beyond the basics, stipulating that dogs be proficient in off-lead obedience, agility, retrieving, small and large article searches, and drug detection prior to certifying or validating a handler-dog team.

Some extremely dangerous situations facing police officers, especially those involving violent and street crime, are the very episodes in which trained handler-dog teams are the most effective: robberies and burglaries in progress, and the searches which may immediately follow such incidents; assaults and prowling incidents; traffic stops where suspects flee stolen cars; and suspicious circumstances. Canines are, also, invaluable in tracking and apprehending suspects or prison escapees and providing backup during the transport of dangerous prisoners. Frequently overlooked is the necessity for patrol officers, working in conjunction with dog handlers during long treks or area searches, to be physically fit enough to keep pace as the canine team moves quickly over rugged terrain. A dog and handler, outrunning their backup, become extremely vulnerable to attack. The canine, with that amazing nose and acute hearing, frequently can find and neutralize perpetrators that several officers working without a dog would never find, despite searching expansively at great risk.

A canine is not only trained to track, chase, and apprehend fleeing lawbreakers, but to protect his handler, without a command, in certain volatile circumstances. This propensity towards handler protection makes the dog an excellent backup in a number of dangerous police encounters where an officer suddenly comes under deadly attack. Some forces use dog-handler teams selectively in crowd control, too. They find that the dog's formidable presence, controlled and directed on a lead to almost any strategic position, can take the spunk out of even the most vocal proponent of mass insurrection at a disturbance. And, if an extremely destructive or violent disorder does start up, dogs can be utilized to remove, one at a time, the most disruptive ringleaders at minimal risk to police and others. A canine can provide decisive backup during an arrest. Rowdy or inebriated roughnecks may think it is macho to punch a cop in front of friends, but even the most drunken social outcast seems to recognize it is senseless to tempt fate by aggravating an intimidating police dog.

Studies show that it is extremely difficult to ambush an officer and a dog working together, as in corporal Wilcott's case. However, if a sneak-attack or sucker-punch should occur, the dog will instantly cast himself into the fracas, probably before the handler has time to react. Then, after the scuffle, the canine will backup the officer during the arrest, guarding at the time of the pat-down and finally escorting the prisoner to the squad car.

Keeping order in jails and prisons is not easy, but, for several years, trained dogs have helped do so under very difficult circumstances in very bleak surroundings. To prevent the escape of inmates, while economically transporting prisoners from one jail or prison to another, some forces have a police dog ride along as an additional guard. And, it is common knowledge that dogs have proven vital when police must track desperate, and possibly armed, escaped prisoners. One of the most famous escapees brought to justice by canines was James Earl Ray, convicted assassin of Dr. Martin Luther King, Jr., after his 1977 breakout from Brushy Mountain State Penitentiary in Tennessee.

A dog provides excellent protection for an officer working alone. A police dog senses human agitation, and will be on high alert if his partner is placed in a hostile environment. Thanks to a window left rolled down on the nearby squad car at a routine traffic stop, or a remote control door opener activated by the officer, a dog may quickly spring to the aid of a lawman who suddenly finds himself in a desperate struggle. At a high risk felony car stop, the canine can help clear the vehicle, reducing the chances that a secret accomplice, still hiding near or inside the vehicle, will ambush the officer. This is especially critical when the vehicle happens to be a van, truck, recreational vehicle, or mobile home.

Many, but certainly not all, patrol dogs are cross-trained to detect the common illegal drugs like marijuana, hashish, hash oil, cocaine, and heroin. Successful completion of drug cross-training makes a patrol dog much more versatile, nearly indispensable in fact, especially to a department that does not have access to a drug-sniffing canine from a neighboring agency.

Random acts of terror, like the catastrophic bombings at New York City's World Trade Center, the Oklahoma City Murrah Federal Office Building, and the passenger airliners blown from the sky, create an ever increasing demand for dogs cross-trained in explosives detection. Even in less-populated areas of the United States and Canada, where militia, gang, and white supremacist activities seem to be escalating, such highly specialized dogs can prove invaluable in protecting the public by searching out hidden bombs and, after an incident or arrest, sniffing out explosives related evidence.

During high-stakes tactical operations, such as the 51-day stalemate at the Branch Davidian compound at Waco, Texas, in 1993, or the

Gustafsen Lake, Canada, native stand-off in 1995, law enforcement can benefit from the versatility of trained canines. At Gustafsen Lake, the largest deployment of trained dogs in Canadian history, RCMP handlers and emergency response team-trained dogs worked sentry duty every night: the teams continually patrolled in the forest and secured fringe areas of the police camp to early-detect intruders or booby traps. Teams also tracked heavily armed men who were eluding police. And, when the dispute was settled, more than 20 dogs used their noses to search for weapons and evidence hidden in the native camp.

A trained police canine is not the solution for every law enforcement problem, nor should every force use dogs. In many situations, such as traffic accident investigation, business fraud, computer hacking, or white collar crime, the canine will be of no utility whatsoever. But, in combatting street crime, dogs are highly effective. Working as a canine officer does have at least one unique benefit, as an article in *LongLine*, the publication of the Canadian Police Canine Association, pointed out: "The police dog is the only law enforcement tool which, if taken away from the officer by the suspect, cannot be used against the lawman."

Even today, as we see more violence erupt in the streets and acts of terrorism become almost commonplace, one constant remains: the loyalty of the police canine is absolute and unconditional.

High-Risk Warrant Executions

The need for a well-conceived, carefully planned, systematic approach to high-risk warrant executions is urgent. Seemingly so routine, warrant service is anything but a rote maneuver. A high-risk warrant execution plan should be carefully thought out and implemented in advance of each service. Adequate personnel and equipment, of course, are essential, but so is the preincident assessment of the problems the officers may encounter during service. Lines of fire, visibility, deciding the best time to execute, assigning roles, and assuring supervision are crucial factors, and should not be overlooked.

Preincident planning includes, but is not limited to, an analyses of: (1) what suspects or items are sought; (2) how many suspects are sought, and how heavily armed they may be; (3) their rapsheets;

(4) the nature of the structure they are holed up in and its locale, with an analysis of offensive and defensive cover possibilities; (5) fields of fire; (6) entry ways and exits for both officers and suspects; (7) dwelling interior layout and type of construction; (8) lighting; (9) the neighborhood and neighbors, and whether they are likely to be friendly or hostile towards police, perhaps even helping the suspects resist the warrant service; (10) the relevant information on utilities; (11) photographs of suspects, the area, and the structure; and (12) any locally-known information that would be helpful in strategic planning, and then executing, the high-risk warrant.

Officers must recognize that the advantage in warrant service operations leans towards the suspects, as they are certainly more familiar with the structure's layout, the weapons they have access to, and the character of the neighborhood. Moreover, the suspects know their intentions, whereas officers can only guess as to the resolve of the thugs to fight or flee. Precision and orderliness are the hallmarks of well planned high-risk warrant executions. A coordinated operation, implementing well-thought-out procedures, will help reduce the prospect of bloodshed.

New Dangers from the Drug World

Another major safety concern today, a distressing by-product of the drug culture, is the danger of contracting a serious disease, while arresting and patting-down an otherwise compliant suspect. This danger stems from the number of intravenous drug users and gang-bangers with contaminated hypodermic needles and syringes hidden on their person, often in the cuffs of their pants. With AIDS, hepatitis, and other communicable diseases as well as the danger from the drugs themselves, it is mandatory that all officers receive safety training in the proper and safest frisk and pat-down procedures. A dedicated officer, accidentally contracting an infectious disease from a cooperative, but addicted, suspect would be an unnecessary tragedy of immense proportions. Similar risks emerge as officers search by hand in vehicles which have been used to transport prisoners.

On a related front, darts tainted with HIV positive blood have been fashioned from ball-point pens and on occasion, shot at police. And, in another equally evil, bizarre scenario, razor blades, concealed in suspects' mouths, have been used to slash at officers and corrections personnel. Needless to say, as criminals become more violent, desperate, and cunning, officers need to receive ongoing training in the most up-to-date countermeasures.

Chapter 7

TECHNOLOGY AND EQUIPMENT IMPROVEMENTS

As technology evolves, more and more systems, protective devices, and garments are being created to enhance the safety of citizens, police officers, police cars, headquarters, and jails. Meanwhile, improved bullet-resistant vests, armored vehicles, helmets, special underwear, capture nets, electric shock devices, chemical agents, gas masks, and other items are rapidly finding their way into the marketplace.

Commercial interests have been quick to capitalize on the street scene by introducing equipment with overblown claims of maxi-capability and mini-cost. For years, some police forces have been easy marks for fast-talking peddlers. Too often, the test of time has shown that such highly promoted gear falls short of claims, proves unsafe, and becomes an expensive white elephant relegated to the police storeroom.

Fortunately, there is a reputable agency which tests and evaluates many items manufactured for police and corrections agencies. This is the National Law Enforcement and Corrections Technology Center, known as NLECTC, headquartered in Rockville, Maryland. It is organized within the National Institute of Justice's Office of Science and Technology, the research branch of the United States Department of Justice. Agencies considering an investment in high-tech or protective gear should consult the NLECTC's evaluations prior to making a purchase.

Specialized equipment, including soft body armor, can prove effective when police face varied types of field problems. The gear provides protection from snipers, irate motorists who turn aggressive, fleeing criminals, and other potentially life-threatening adversaries. While equipment and systems can be valuable, equipment alone should never be viewed as a surefire means of protection. Effective, career long training still remains the strongest defense for the always vulnerable police officer.

Dispatching, Telephones, and Computers

Communications centers are lifesaving centers. The emergency personnel, who take calls from citizens and then dispatch officers to the scene, have an immense impact on police safety. The application of computers and sophisticated systems technology enhances officer safety, too.

Improving Radio Dispatching

The backbone of any efficient police department is its radio communications system, which allows officers to instantly communicate with headquarters, with each other, and with supervisory personnel. However, a modern system is only as good as the operators on duty. An incomplete or poorly worded radio dispatch can put an officer at a serious disadvantage. It may even put that individual in a perilous situation if he or she lacks vital information about an assignment, and is unaware of its possible risks. In short, radio dispatchers must work efficiently behind the scenes, sending officers on calls fully alert to any dangers they might expect to find at their destination.

There are two frequent problems inherent in a poor radio dispatch. One is the failure of the dispatcher to relay enough pertinent information to the field officer. This is related to the second problem: the telephone answering staff, if separate from the dispatcher, may fail to obtain enough detail from the complainant to provide sufficient information to prepare the responding officer. Inept or lazy persons handling the phones, as well as unskilled, untrained, or indifferent dispatchers, may unintentionally compromise police safety.

Training programs for personnel who take incoming telephone calls, and for radio dispatchers, must be established and required of all dispatch center personnel. The dispatcher's job, although technically a desk job, is far from boring. He or she must remain calm when speaking with the public, even callers who are under extraordinary stress or are panicked to the point of near irrationality. Once basic details have been secured, the dispatcher must clearly and concisely send one or more units to the incident, briefing them as to the anticipated circumstances. Whether or not the critical information is accurately and professionally relayed will determine, to a large extent, the success of the field officer in carrying out the assignment.

The training of telephone and dispatching personnel should include some time in the field, observing firsthand the importance of the work they perform. Staff should be obliged to ride with officers on patrol so they can more fully appreciate the consequences of misinterpretation, misinformation, or too little information. In this way, dispatchers will better understand the significance of their own position and appreciate the risks inherent in inadequate or sloppy communication. Communications personnel must also understand that there should never be any question in the patrol officer's mind as to the nature of the call, its location and what circumstances apply.

Let's examine the impact of poor communication when it is translated into operational terms. Take, for instance, a radio dispatch directing police to proceed to 1234 Elm to "take a call from a woman," or, perhaps "from a man." With only that information, an officer is inadequately prepared to safely deal with the call, especially if it turns out to be a domestic disturbance with a dangerous weapon in the hands of the spouse. Typically, an officer would perceive "a call from a woman or man" to mean that he or she wishes to discuss a traffic matter, report a theft, or needs advice of some sort. It is assumed to be routine and not threatening, so no special precautions would be taken. And, there is little or no chance that a nearby unit would provide backup. Dispatchers must be reminded that a wary officer, early-warned by radio, is less susceptible to skulduggery than one that is uninformed and ill-prepared.

As police are human, there is no sure way to keep an officer mentally alert to all possible dangers in a given situation. But, to improve his or her odds of survival, it is essential that the most complete information be available from the communications center.

Improved dispatching procedures are important in all field operations. They are especially crucial when police are being sent to a robbery or burglary alarm, calls involving heavy drinkers and the mentally unstable, a felony in progress, or a domestic disturbance. In any hot case, all responding units should be assigned to specific duties and be advised of the relevant details and the nature of the report, insofar as they may be known. Vastly improved telephone answering and radio dispatching procedures and the use of a standard dispatching signal code will, hopefully, lead to greater officer awareness, hence safety.

There is an additional element required to assure the finest possible radio dispatching: street cops must be sympathetic to the problems dispatchers face and understand what the job involves. Therefore, street cops in training should be obliged to observe the dispatch center staff at work. Better yet, if circumstances allow, officers should be required to work dispatch on occasion.

The dispatcher occupies a pivotal position in contributing to police safety. On the one hand, the dispatcher should remain emotionally uninvolved in the personal activities of officers and emergency callers, while simultaneously being concerned, perceptive, inquiring and professional. These qualities are best fostered through extensive dispatcher training, coupled with experience and on-the-job evaluation. Yet, training a dispatcher or an operator better, is but one immediate step which can provide an officer on patrol with quicker, more complete information about a call. Today, there are state-of-the-art products on the market that should lead to officer safety through improved communication.

Combined Communications

More and more forces are amalgamating telephone and radio communications so that a single, sophisticated, well-equipped center can serve the needs of a region. Centralized dispatch can assure that all forces in a geographical area, including very small ones, have around-the clock service. A coordinated system can eliminate the overlap, confusion and duplication so common to individual systems in a region. A region wide operation is cost efficient, as it maximizes the number of dispatch personnel, makes their training easier and accommodates a 911 emergency telephone system. The virtues of combined communications and records-keeping are many and can contribute to a higher degree of safety for police.

Electronic Processing Systems

Computers are being used by several large forces to decrease the time required to process calls. For example, in one system the dispatcher types the address of an urgent call onto a video terminal. Within moments, a computer verifies the address and gives a geographical location. The distress call is beamed to the nearest patrol cars where it is displayed on a video screen for the officers to read. Within seconds, police should acknowledge the call and be on their way.

This equipment cuts down the chance that an officer will make an error in writing down a radio call. With less chance of a mistake in communications, there is less chance of ending up at the wrong location, getting the wrong read on a situation, or worse yet, going to a dangerous call unprepared. Officers are less likely to become victims when vehicle license plates and names can be checked, with enquiries being fully processed by a computer and speedily returned to the field.

Another computer-based police dispatching system offers immediate response when an emergency call is received by the dispatcher. While most of a department's calls for assistance are routine, when an emergency comes in, it gets top priority. Time is critical when recording and dispatching pertinent emergency information to a responding officer.

When a call for assistance is received, a police complaint operator asks a few key questions, then types the address into a computer-aided dispatching system. Once polled, the computer immediately indicates the "street to beat" response sequence. It links the address with the proper motor patrol area, census tract, and radio frequency of the assignment. This information appears on the video monitor of the dispatcher handling that frequency, along with the status of all units available for dispatch. After assigning the units, the dispatcher clears the screen and handles the next highest priority call.

Another computer application keeps officers on the street and enhances their safety. This is E-mail, whereby police may file investigative reports and communicate with other stations and officers without leaving the street. E-mail allows officers to use their time efficiently, and virtually eliminates the need to write reports at headquarters. E-mail, as a system, underscores that, in the future, technology will bring many innovations to law enforcement!

Electronic Car Locators

Electronic car locators help save police lives. An incident involving a highway patrol trooper, slain on a lonely country road, is illustrative. The dispatcher had no information on the whereabouts of the trooper or his patrol car, except that he had been stopping an auto somewhere. A few frenzied hours later, after a tip from an alert motorist, police converged on a tragic scene: the trooper was dead, the patrol car's roof lights still flashing.

What time had the murder been committed? Were any people or cars seen on the road shortly after the shooting? Investigators were unable to answer any of these questions since the trooper had failed to report into headquarters. In this type of incident, a car locator system is of premium value.

If the department had integrated an electronic car locator into its dispatching center, the communications personnel would have been able to quickly locate the trooper and his car. As it was, substantial time elapsed before the magnitude of the disaster became known, which may explain why it took seven months before a suspect was taken into custody.

An electronic car locator system will enhance officer safety. It is designed so each mobile unit has an emergency status button that can provide an electronic alert to a department's communications center. Officers in need of help may instantly specify their location and status, without relying on voice communications. The digital system reduces voice transmission and decreases radio channel congestion by up to 33 percent, further promoting officer safety by freeing air time for urgent voice messages. Without such a system, it is crucial that each officer quickly and accurately write down the location of any call and then sign off. The radio frequencies must remain clear for other urgent police business.

Another major advantage of computer communications and non-voice systems, is the privacy they provide. With the proliferation of low-cost scanners, the safety of patrol officers has been jeopardized. It is not uncommon for burglars and rings of thieves to monitor local police frequencies, then flee the scene as soon as they hear any reference to the address of the home or business they are plundering. Police have many different codes, which can be changed, but it is difficult to dispatch a unit without at least giving out the location of the emergency.

Ideally, departments in high-crime metropolitan areas should handle all critical communications with either a computer system or, another alternative, a voice privacy scrambler radio, as used in many undercover, tactical, and narcotics operations.

Whether it is an emergency or carelessness that causes an officer to fail to radio in his or her position, strategically, it is best if that location can be pinpointed at a moment's notice. And since it is advantageous to dispatch the nearest squad car in an emergency, the car locator system allows for greater patrol efficiency and timesaving.

Personal Portable Radio Gear

It is common for officers to be routinely equipped with portable personal radios. These modern hand-held transceivers are among the most-important-ever innovations in police communications equipment. On a daily basis they prove their merit in facilitating police operations and enhancing safety.

The advantages are noteworthy. When equipped with a radio, a patrol officer on foot or a bicycle, or patrolling on foot away from his or her patrol car, is no longer out of touch with the communications center or nearby backup. In some gunfire incidents, where the officer has been away from his patrol car's radio, a call for assistance on the portable unit has proven to be more of a lifesaver than a service revolver.

Portable radios offer other safety advantages. For example, if an officer spots a wanted suspect, instead of feeling obliged to make a single-handed effort at capture, a request for backup from other units in the area is fast and efficient. Clearly, this is prudence, made possible by the compactness, convenience and safety inherent in portable radio gear. The instrument may be carried in the hand, as a walkie-talkie, or easily affixed to the officer's uniform. The microphone/speaker monitor may be attached to the shoulder, with the transceiver secured to the belt. Such gear is sufficiently lightweight so as not to cause undue discomfort or encumbrance.

911: A National Emergency Phone Number

In the 1990s, there has been a steady movement to implement a national emergency police number, the 911 system. Despite progress in the United States and Canada, the concept is by no means fully embraced. It should be, for the 911 system has been shown to save lives, both citizens and police officers.

The value of having but one emergency number across a nation is evident. It could lead to dispatching police, and other emergency personnel, to trouble calls more quickly than ever before. Often a quick response keeps situations from deteriorating further, making a more extensive police intervention at a later time unnecessary. Once a situation becomes violent, the risk to the safety and well-being of everyone increases. A standardized national emergency number could reduce response time to nonviolent crimes as well. That betters the odds of catching suspects in the act, thus removing from the street criminals who, later, may resort to violence against police.

Another advantage of a single emergency number is to facilitate direct communication between the complainant and the police dispatcher. Most citizens can remember a three digit, nationally consistent number and would call it directly instead of phoning the telephone operator in an emergency. Trained police personnel could obtain better information for the responding officer, instead of having to depend on the memory of a harried phone company employee.

Communications and computer technology is such that a 911 system can be upgraded to provide personnel with access to the caller's address and phone number, without asking a single question. It could also be programmed to display the name of the resident or business, type of phone—home or apartment, office, coin—and the nearest police, fire or ambulance unit. These remarkable lifesaving possibilities are included in the Enhanced 911 system, called E-911 in those places that have opted for these features.

There are some issues which must be resolved when a community contemplates the implementation of a 911 or an E-911 telephone system. Who will pay for it and according to what formula? Also, to what extent, if any, will state or federal funds be made available? One means of allocating costs, when the system is set up to serve a region, is to bill participating agencies a percentage of the total cost, based on the population served.

After cost issues have been resolved, there is an urgent need to educate the public as to the operation of the system, what it is for and, importantly, what it is not for. Concurrently, communications personnel must be trained in the system, its goals and mechanics. Each department must make sure that it has sufficient backup equipment and an emergency power source to provide redundancy during any power outages.

The Baltimore, Maryland, Police Department implemented a two-year pilot project in the fall of 1996 to test whether a NONemergency telephone number—311—would relieve the overburdened 911 operators. If the Baltimore demonstration project is successful, and the public takes to the system, 311 could be a simple and easy-to-remember number for citizens to report noncritical situations to police. Since the U.S. Justice Department expects the project will prove worthwhile, the agency has requested the Federal Communications Commission reserve 311, to be used nationwide for nonemergency calls.

Another troublesome issue is being evaluated as police in southern New Jersey implement a program to see if they can trace the precise location of a person who calls 911 from a cellular phone. The experimental technology began a 90-day trial run in early 1997. If all goes as hoped, by late 2001 it should make no difference to an E-911 system what kind of phone a person used to call police—the crew at the dispatch center will know your location.

Computerized Information Systems

There has been a need for a system that could help police early identify hostility at traffic stops and other police-citizen contacts. This has resulted in the development of several computer-based information systems patterned after the FBI's National Crime Information Center (NCIC). The FBI computer contains information on badly wanted felons, stolen cars, hot guns, and so forth. It is a nationwide system, with a high threshold of entry, which means it focuses on federal offenders and not on most local crimes and wants. In Canada, the Canadian Police Information Center (CPIC) serves a similar purpose, and is linked with the NCIC.

There is a need for regional and local computer-based information systems of a lower threshold of entry, providing local information and wants. Such systems have been designed as backup for the NCIC and are operational in several locales. The greater Kansas City area is served by a highly advanced computer-based police information system called ALERT, an acronym for the Automated Law Enforcement

Response Team. The Kansas City network was designed to keep local records of stolen vehicles, wanted persons, aliases used by criminals, current lists of fugitives, and crime reporting statistics. The system makes this information readily available to police upon local inquiry. The Kansas City system is interfaced with the FBI's NCIC in Washington, D.C.

Several other locally-based systems can be designed to supplement the NCIC and ALERT type networks. These include an automated firearm system, an automated property system, a stolen vehicle system, a wanted persons system, a criminal history system, and a police information network. The possibilities are endless!

When automated information systems are utilized, there must be training to enable staff to quickly access the data banks. Officers must be computer-literate and proficient in polling those resources which are available to aid them in performing their duties. As more and more computers are being integrated into law enforcement, an up-to-date inventory of all the various systems, as well as their purpose and availability, is indispensable.

Body Protective Equipment

The concept of protecting one's body by virtue of a shield, or specially designed apparel, is as old as war. Police have need for such armor because of the nature of their role. Spurred by the massive disorders of the 60s and 70s, and by the way the streets are in the 1990s, the protective equipment industry has been on a research, development and marketing binge. This has led to numerous products, some of them now standard equipment, which help protect officers.

Bullet-Resistant Vests and Jackets

A majority of officers murdered on duty are victims of gunshot wounds in the upper chest or upper back, areas which would have been protected by bullet-resistant vests, had they been wearing them. Ironically, some victims were wearing soft body armor, but took hits in areas just barely beyond that covered by the garments, such as under the arm, in the neck line, or the lower abdomen. Notwithstanding these exceptions, bullet-resistant vests and jackets have become lifesavers in a big way, and if more officers would wear them there would be fewer casualties.

A few years ago, a motorcycle officer, on an impulse, purchased body armor. Soon after, the investment saved his life: the vest stopped a bullet, shot by a motorist during an apparently routine traffic stop. Two weeks later, another officer's life was spared when a motorist fired directly at his heart. Both officers were left with bruises, but they survived! Soon after these incidents, the city council made bullet resistant vests standard equipment for that city's 7,000 police. While the vests were expensive, this purchase proved to be highly cost-effective in terms of officer safety and morale, time on the job saved from injury-related absences, and medical and pension benefit expenditures.

For years, departments across the nation have sought a lightweight, undetectable, yet comfortable, bullet-resistant vest. In 1974, the Law Enforcement Assistance Administration started overseeing the preparation of lightweight and inconspicuous protective garments for law enforcement. The garments used a synthetic fabric, called Kevlar, which today has been integrated into police uniforms or made into a separate vest. The LEAA contracted with the Aerospace Corporation of El Segundo, California, to fabricate the vests and run a series of ballistic and related tests.

Tests conducted on the Kevlar fabric concluded that it was a highly efficient protective material. When fashioned into a jacket or vest, it has been shown to protect against 30 percent of guns of all types tested, and was even more effective against blunt shots fired from 90 to 95 percent of all handguns common in the United States. Other companies, also, have developed ballistic materials, which has opened up the market and created more equipment options for police.

The decision of whether or not to employ or provide bullet-resistant vests, of course, rests with the administration of each department. However, every police and sheriff's department should be familiar with the availability of these garments and should evaluate their usefulness based upon local street conditions. At today's prices, a quality vest, National Institute of Justice-certified, costs about $400.

As criminals become more cunning, police officers are running into more suspects wearing body armor. Back in the 1980s, the Elmira, New York, police found themselves in a shootout with two armor-clad kidnapping suspects. One man was killed by police return-fire, while the second committed suicide. Both suspects were heavily armed. The mortally wounded perpetrator was one of those individuals unlucky enough to sustain a fatal wound in an area that was unprotected by the vest.

At first, the stumbling block was persuading officers to wear body armor. Although current models weigh but a few pounds, the vests are hot and confining and may cause some discomfort. If a department requires its personnel to wear protective armor, preparations must be taken to ease a resultant problem: the garments may produce loss of body salt and excessive perspiration, especially during hot weather. Officers, alert to the problem, should consider supplementing their salt intake with tablets. The department may advise officers of the necessity to take seasonal precautionary measures prescribed by the public health physician.

Riot Helmets and Other Body Armor

The Law Enforcement Standards Program was created as a result of the Omnibus Crime Control and Safe Streets Act of 1968 and was designed to develop and test new and improved techniques, systems and equipment. Its standard for a police riot helmet declared: ". . . they [the helmets] are not generally designed to offer protection against gunfire." The need for a protective helmet is readily apparent on certain assignments, such as in strike or riot control duty, flushing out gunmen, at hostage-taking incidents and during barricades and roadblocks. They may also be useful during raids.

Helmets, though, tend to be uncomfortable when worn for long periods and may restrict an officer's vision and movement. But, where a specific risk is anticipated, such as rioters throwing rocks and bricks, wearing a helmet makes sense.

Helmets must be designed to protect against blows to the side or the top of the head. A good, utilitarian helmet is similar to a motorcycle helmet. The visor, unless the officer is wearing protective goggles instead, must have good impact strength, while being made of a clear plastic, lightweight material. There must be adequate ventilation, along with a form of stripping which will prevent liquids from running into the helmet and onto the officer's face.

Research is also underway in the area of bullet-resistant face shields, bullet-resistant groin and leg protectors, and even full body armor and shields. Clearly, it is neither practical nor desirable for officers to routinely wear such apparel, as the military appearance conveyed would surely upset public sensibilities. However, when seeking a sniper, waiting out a hostage incident or a barricaded criminal, wearing body armor or taking cover behind a shield is logical.

De-Militarizing Police Officer Appearance

Rather than adopting defensive apparel, at one time some forces put their street cops in sportcoats or blazers to soothe potentially dangerous police-citizen encounters. No longer wearing the traditional dark uniforms, officers so clad hardly looked like typical men-in-blue. These departments sought to change their image by projecting a sense of a police "service" rather than a police "force."

In terms of protective clothing, the blazers were intended to blunt the outright hostility the traditional uniform incites in some people. Whether or not the jackets had the desired effect is speculative, but the innovation underscores the theory that an officer's uniform and appearance may antagonize some people.

In a similar, but less dramatic move in the late sixties, many police departments had shoulder patch replicas of the American flag sewn on their uniforms. Some forces put a flag decal on police vehicles, too. The trend began as a silent protest to the disrespect shown the national colors by draft protestors, campus agitators, and flag-burners. Some police officials believe that the patriotic gesture created goodwill with the general public and discouraged assaults on officers.

Dressing in blazers, or wearing patriotic symbols, were responses by police administrators who had become alarmed by violent, anti-police aggression. These measures were intended to portray police as interested in serving the public without encouraging disobedience or compromising officer safety. Although the results were inconclusive, more research is justified.

Special Detection Devices

It is a fact of life that incidents do occur in which the only safe course of action available to police is justifiable homicide. Take, for example, the sniper who has positioned himself strategically and is firing randomly on citizens. It may be that the only reasonable option is to have a police sharpshooter fire at the sniper, which is unfortunate. It is even more unfortunate that, in handling such incidents, police often lack the sophisticated weaponry and detection equipment necessary to expeditiously complete the job.

Historically, in sniper attacks, authorities have tried to flush out or neutralize an entrenched gunman by using a canine unit or a tactical team. But one problem which consistently plagues police is pinpointing the exact location of a hidden gunman. Law enforcement needs access to searching devices, that have the capacity to uncover a sniper soon after he has taken overt action. Many different technologies have been developed to achieve this objective. But typically, tools of this nature are more available to the armed forces or the larger federal policing agencies, than to civilian police departments. It is obvious that having access to this type of equipment would provide strategic and safety benefits for all police.

In particular, night-vision devices give law enforcement the upper hand by enabling a search of hallways, dark alleys, and fields and streets without sacrificing an officer's protective cover. Rugged and lightweight optics which can achieve this objective, although readily available, are still too pricey to be standard equipment in every patrol car. However, any sophisticated drug squad, SWAT, or ERT team must have at its disposal an array of versatile night vision gear, including goggles, binoculars, scopes, and camera lenses. In a short time, this equipment is likely to become less expensive, as more night vision products are being manufactured for the price-driven consumer market.

In the future, an affordable instrument which will sense body heat or some other metabolic process is needed so police may quickly detect the presence of a human being in hiding. Such a device would be useful, in both the daytime and at night, for locating a suspect hunkered down in a parking lot, a backyard, out in the woods, or even inside a building.

Infrared search and detection devices, that sense body heat, are in limited use today. A more expensive unit manufactured for professional surveillance will detect a person's "infrared signature" as long as he or she is not hiding in or behind cover that is too dense. Again, as with night vision goggles, high per-unit-costs make it prohibitive for most police departments to purchase a quality infrared for every squad car. And, the less expensive units being sold in consumer catalogs are not yet of a quality suitable for police work.

So far, a device that can actually peer through walls—useful to help identify the position of a terrorist, kidnapper, sniper, or a hostage—is more elusive.

Scientists and defense contractors, utilizing the electro-magnetic spectrum—infrared, millimeter, ultraviolet and x-rays, as well as laser vibration detectors—have developed surveillance and eavesdropping equipment of a very sophisticated nature. But, as much of this technologically advanced equipment is top-secret and classified by the government, it is used almost exclusively by the military, federal law enforcement agencies, and elite anti-terrorist teams.

One highly sophisticated infrared device has found its way into police use, at least with some large forces that utilize aircraft. FLIR, which stands for forward-looking infrared, was originally designed many years ago for the military. Today, it is used by some large metropolitan forces and federal police agencies, including the FBI, the U.S. Customs Service, and the Royal Canadian Mounted Police which maintain their own fleet of helicopters. FLIR sensors allow the pilot and crew to track or search at great distances for cars, planes, boats, or other objects that emit heat, including humans and animals. A thermal image is displayed on a separate monitor, or even on a screen inside the pilot's flight helmet.

Hopefully, one day, even more state-of-the-art surveillance and reconnaissance equipment, designed for military use, will be affordable for the police. Such gear can save lives, especially during hostage-taking, kidnapping, and dangerous SWAT or ERT missions.

High-powered rifles, with scopes, night vision devices and extensive fine sighting equipment, are essential for those occasions when suspects have isolated themselves and taken the lives of others. If a department lacks the funding for weaponry, prior arrangements should be made to secure access to the gear from the state, a nearby force, or from a military facility in the vicinity, together with the personnel skilled in its use.

Law enforcement agencies urgently need sophisticated tactical equipment. Without it, police administrators risk a regrettable situation: the murder of their own officers and, possibly, the deaths of innocent citizens.

Chapter 8

TWO SPECIAL ENTERPRISES: JAILING AND UNDERCOVER ROLES

Undercover work has always been hazardous and continues to be. Jailing is also a hazardous role but has never been adequately identified as such. Steps, set out in this chapter, can be taken to minimize the danger to personnel serving in these roles.

The Jail Can Be a Dangerous Place

Keeping a suspect within a confined area, such as in the security section of a jail or lockup, is far more hazardous than most people imagine. It is easy to assume that suspects are subdued and under control by the time police get them to a jail or prison. This simply isn't so, as seemingly contrite prisoners can suddenly burst into a physical frenzy, catching the staff off-guard. Attacks on officers, which occur in supposedly secure areas, should be of major concern to police administrators. In a sense, custody is a game of chess between prisoners and officers.

There are two reasons why an already secure area can be so dangerous. First, detention personnel across the nation may be victimized by handmade weapons, some crude, others ingenious, but either can be very deadly. The second is even more dangerous. It is that desperate inmates may become ruthless should they seek to escape. Taken together, the two factors constitute an ever-present danger to corrections personnel in county jails and city lockups as well as in state penitentiaries.

Remarkably, none of the 61 Oklahoma police officer murder study victims was killed during a breakout or an incident in a jail or lockup.

But five perpetrators, who had escaped from prison or jail, and six others being transported there, combined to murder 12 of the 61 officers from 1950 through 1994. Clearly, police have a stake in the safety and security aspects of detention facilities, as well as the transport of prisoners.

Even though no Oklahoma police were killed during jail or prison breakouts, it should not be assumed that breakouts are outdated, or that the county jails and city lockups are so secure that escape is impossible. On the contrary: some rural jails and city lockups throughout the United States are extremely vulnerable to cunning prisoners planning an escape.

Circumstances in Jails and Lockups

County jails and city lockups are at least as hazardous to the police who staff them as state prisons are to correctional officers. Serious inmate overcrowding and poor physical facilities are two leading contributors to this dangerous situation.

In spite of jail standards, there are still some ancient facilities that are poorly maintained, were not even well-designed initially, and fall below nationally accepted standards of custody. A few are so old that cell doors, including those housing felony suspects, are secured only by chains and padlocks! And some jails across America have inadequate medical facilities, if any at all, and several have inadequate toilet facilities. Finally, many jails have neither exercise nor recreation areas for prisoners, and inmates are so crowded that the staff is unable to segregate classes of prisoners or effectively keep gangs apart. And equally as troubling, sometimes space limitations force the administration to house mentally ill persons among the general inmate population, creating a potentially explosive condition.

The National Institute of Corrections reports that, in 1994, there were 3,272 county jails in the United States. In addition, there were at least 228 city jails, also called adult detention facilities, and there are thousands of smaller lockups in which prisoners may be detained for short periods while awaiting court or interrogation.

The Bureau of Justice Statistics reports that in 1995, there were 507,044 persons held in the nation's jails, and about 165,500 staff employed in these facilities. About one out of every eight jails had some type of in-house medical facility, although, in relative terms, such facilities were commonplace only in large institutions. Slightly more than three of every five jails provided inmates with some form of recreation or entertainment. Such diversions were highly limited, except in large institutions, and were absent in many small and medium sized jails.

Overcrowding joins obsolescence as being a pernicious jail problem nationwide. But there has been movement toward easing both problems. In 1995, 93 percent of jail capacity was occupied across the nation, after having been at a record 108 percent in 1989. However, since 1989, rated capacity has risen by nearly 178,000 beds, while the number of inmates has increased just 112,000. Even though jails are at less than capacity, there are still lots of people in areas too small to accommodate them, especially in those facilities which are old and deteriorating. It creates a dangerous environment for inmates and staff alike.

There are troubles related to overcrowding in state prisons across the nation, too, which, in 1995, held about 950,000 prisoners. Like some county jails, there are certain state prisons which are very old. In December, 1995, state prison systems were operating between 14 and 25 percent over their reported capacity, and the federal system was operating 26 percent over its reported capacity. These conditions have prompted many state penal systems to send some of their inmates to county jails in order to ease overcrowding. Clearly, this makes jails even more dangerous places for the less-hardened inmates and staff alike.

There are three factors in county jails and city lockups which are alarming when considered in terms of officer safety. First, and it is hard to believe even today, some personnel are part-time, untrained employees. Second, not all full-time jail and lockup employees have received sufficient training in custody, security procedures and searching. Third, many street cops are familiar with the jail or lockup only insofar as the booking process is involved; they haven't a clue to the procedures and nuances involved in safely serving as staff in a detention setting when called upon to do so. Yet, there are occasions when street cops find themselves assigned for a day, a week or some other short-term period to serve at the jail. This terribly dangerous practice happens because jail security, in contrast to patrol, requires that a certain number of mandatory positions be staffed on a regular basis.

When there are insufficient correctional staff, patrol officers may be assigned to jailing roles. The danger of such a practice is illuminated by an analogy: surely a sheriff or police chief would not ask an untrained detention officer to serve, even a single day, on patrol duty, because it is obvious that the employee would be at risk and would put others at risk as well.

Since most police patrol officers are neither trained in jailing, nor motivated to serve there, street officers look upon even one day of jail duty as "eight hours in Siberia." To them, it is a stigma post.

Most officers murdered, while on jail duty, were patrol or detective personnel who, while booking prisoners, were surprise attacked. The attacks usually occurred after handcuffs were removed and the suspect sensed that the moment of truth had arrived. Exacerbating the situation was the fact that so many suspects being booked had been drinking heavily, or had ingested illegal drugs, which may have contributed to their being arrested in the first place.

Nonauthorized weapons of any sort inside a jail or lockup are a surefire invitation to mayhem. This especially applies to firearms, those which patrol or detective personnel bear in the course of their duties outside the penal facility. Yet, dismayingly, there are still some forces which allow officers and detectives to routinely bear their firearms, batons, or chemical weapons while in the jail security sector, including while booking prisoners! This practice is inexcusably careless and is an invitation to gun-grabbing and shooting incidents. The message is that unsecured firearms and other street weapons in jail facilities violates every principle of accepted jail management and police procedure.

In some facilities, both the age and location of the jail within the headquarters building contributed to assaults on officers. For example, one city had its jail located so that the female detention area was clearly visible to anyone passing through. When male prisoners were brought into the station for booking, an inordinate number of assaults took place as the men were led past the women. Male suspects were showing off their machismo by attacking officers in front of the females.

Police administrators should place priority on making jail facilities secure, thus reducing escapes and jail disorders. But most problems are not related to physical design, but human carelessness, linked to a lack of training and supervision, or to jail personnel failing to adhere to safety procedures. Clearly, it is essential that personnel assigned to jail roles should receive thorough training and regular retraining in safety and security. This training should be provided for all personnel, including commanders, and even staff subject to short-term relief assignments. And, the training should be completed *before* the employees assume their jail duties.

Many counties and cities have failed to dedicate adequate funds for upgrading county jails and city lockups. Yet the social and political pressures on sheriffs and police chiefs to upgrade, reconstruct, and expand prisoner facilities have intensified. Demands are being made to provide rehabilitation programs and services for convicted prisoners. Periodic state and federal inspections, the adoption of jail standards, court mandates, and sometimes local grand jury reports, force issues of prisoner confinement into the public eye.

One means of addressing the dangers inherent in jails and lockups is to embrace measures intended to reduce county jail admissions and to speed the release of nonviolent offenders. Sheriffs, police chiefs, and judges should meet and develop plans for safer facilities and improved programs. Innovations such as house arrest, drug courts, and electronic monitoring of nonviolent offenders show promise, while at the same time not compromising community and officer safety. And congestion in jails would be reduced if judges would issue orders expeditiously moving convicted prisoners to the state penitentiary, assuming there is space there, soon after sentencing.

It is also timely for those counties, facing the need to build new jails, to confer with nearby cities about whether a joint facilities arrangement can be worked out, so one jail can serve an urbanized area. Resource pooling makes fiscal sense, appears efficient in handling prisoners, capitalizes on economies of scale, and enhances recruitment, training, and retention of professional custodial staff. Moreover, jail consolidation has been consistently encouraged by respected government study groups, and, in most places where a regional jail has been opened, it has worked out well.

Jail consolidation is neither new nor unusual. Cleveland County, Oklahoma, handles all of the prisoners for the cities of Norman and Moore; Goodhue County and Red Wing, Minnesota, have merged jails; as have the forces of Reno and Sparks with Washoe County, Nevada. Some other prominent examples where cities have merged their jails with counties are found in Phoenix and Maricopa County,

Arizona; Miami and Dade County, Florida; and Tucson and Pima County, Arizona. The amalgamation of jails may not solve every problem, but the move should help improve security, minimize costs, and reduce attacks on detention officers.

There is a trend emerging which finds some cities in urban areas getting back into jailing. One of the reasons seems to be a knee-jerk reaction, because political figures are clamoring for police to arrest those persons whose behavior constitutes nuisance-type misdemeanors like littering, panhandling, prostitution, loitering, and sleeping in unauthorized places. This extremely expensive trend may ease political pressures on the politicians and police, but it does nothing to make officers safer.

Some state corrections systems have formed a special unit which goes into service as soon as a jail break has been detected. This team of investigators, working fulltime to track the escapee, begins by talking with persons who have visited, written, or phoned the inmate. Major focus is placed on the escapee's family and those friends who have been phoned most often and most recently by the prisoner. An impressive array of intelligence is often crucial to swiftly recapturing suspects, before they have a chance to go into deep hiding or get into additional trouble. Very large county jails may form similar units, ready for quick action, when an escape is detected.

Special units can serve many purposes, other than the standard post escape work. Members of these units can handle or isolate violent prisoners, and can oversee their transportation to court, the hospital, or to prison. They also prove valuable when disturbances erupt in jail recreation areas, in dormitories, drunk tanks, or other areas of the institution.

Searching for Contraband

Surprising as it may seem, there is an inmate culture in most prisons and jails across America which includes, among other activities, a booming business in contraband. It is an organizational phenomenon in jails that facilitates the contraband problem. Essentially, the powerful inmates or gangs control both the prison social structure and the contraband trade. Watch-dogging the inmate culture and bringing the illegal prison and jail market system to heel is not easy to do, but some standard procedures may reduce the flow of contraband in institutions.

Personnel in every prison, jail, or lockup should conduct periodic, but not predictable or prescheduled, comprehensive searches for contraband. Vehicles in which prisoners are transported, rooms in which they are questioned, and cells where they await court appearances should be shaken down often, on unannounced occasions. Searches should include inmate living and recreation areas, cells, and common shower and toilet areas. And no jail or lockup should overlook the prospect that contraband may enter the facility by means of visitors and letters and packages sent to inmates through the United States mail.

Increasingly, jails have programs whereby prisoners work outside the institution, returning to the facility for supper and overnight. By way of work-release programs, public works-type laboring roles, and cleanup squads which make parks and waterways more attractive, inmates have unlimited opportunities to scavenge all sorts of items, many of which are not welcome inside the jail. This means that every time a prisoner leaves the institution, for whatever reason, he or she should be thoroughly searched before being re-admitted. Too often the staff conduct such searches perfunctorily, which is careless.

Items discovered during searches are usually routine, but they can spell trouble. Such simple objects as pencils, combs, and mess hall utensils might, when sharpened, become weapons. A paper clip or a ball point pen plastic cartridge may be fashioned to pick handcuff locks. Occasionally, innovative contraband turns up, illustrating the inventiveness, cunning, and determination born of desperation among people in custody. A full array of dangerous weapons and replicas, some crudely fashioned, others beautifully tooled, may be uncovered. Sweeping searches are important for the safety not just of jail personnel, but for the safety of other inmates and visitors.

Some jails and prisons have formed specialized security squads to fight the increasing problem of contraband. These units ferret out thousands of items each year, including many dangerous weapons. These squads are essential since measures associated with the ordinary security routine of an institution rarely cope with the ingenuity inmates show in handcrafting weapons. In addition to weapons, specialized security squads sometimes discover escape-kits which include grapples, ropes and saws. Other common contraband includes cash, pills, narcotics, and "pruno," potent alcohol made in very ingenious secret stills. Specialized security squad members, which may include booze and drug-sniffing dogs, may play another role, by giving inservice training to corrections personnel and then reporting on the physical security of prisons, jails and lockups.

Since many jails serve counties which are not heavily populated, there may be justification to form a specialized security squad which serves institutions on a regional basis. Squad members could, also, train local corrections and police personnel in the more intricate nuances of booking, jailing and the care and custody of prisoners. As a practical matter, if a state opted to provide this service, the team could be based at a regional state penitentiary and be funded as part of the corrections budget. This concept is but one of many measures intended to make jails and lockups safer places for staff, inmates, and visitors.

Electronic and Systems Applications to Jail Security

There are hundreds of very good electronic devices and systems which can be made part of the physical plant, thus enhancing the safety of corrections personnel and prisoners. The array of devices and systems should be carefully evaluated in view of specific requirements, on an institution by institution basis. The problem is, there is no single system or application that fits all institutions, as each location and inmate population has unique characteristics. Hence, the latest technology should be carefully evaluated and selectively screened, remembering that there is certainly a place for the proper alarms and devices in any detention facility.

Pretrial Diversion Programs

As shown in Chapter 3, it is not unusual that suspects accused of murdering police have been arrested prior to the fatal incident. Yet, by no means did a conviction always follow the earlier arrest. These cases fell out of the judicial system for many reasons, such as insufficient evidence, the nature of the crime, prosecutorial discretion, and plea bargaining.

Clearly, there exists a need for viable alternatives to incarcerating persons suspected of nonviolent minor crimes. Prison is but a breeding ground for more crime. Yet incarceration is the usual form of disposition for many run-of-the-mill, petty offenders, but in many instances it is not necessarily the best alternative.

A process called pretrial diversion is an alternative to either prosecuting or dismissing charges. Used on the state and local levels for many years, it has been introduced at the federal level. In such a program, law-breakers are offered a chance to avoid trial and the stigma of a permanent criminal record if they satisfactorily complete an individually tailored, preplanned rehabilitation program. Thus, federal and state prosecutors grant certain offenders, whom they feel are not likely to become repeat offenders, the opportunity to take part in a closely supervised, community-based rehabilitation program. The suspect, upon advice of defense counsel, signs a contract with the court agreeing to take part in the voluntary program for a fixed period and with specific conditions, for up to a year. The offender waives the right to a speedy trial and the statute of limitations on the offense, which is the prosecution's hedge in the event the offender violates the agreement. Participation in the program is neither an admission of guilt, nor are records admissible in court.

The advantages of pretrial diversion programs in preventing assaults on police are long-range. If nonviolent offenders, in pretrial diversion programs, live up to the terms, they are less likely to commit crimes in the future. On the other hand, if these suspects go to trial, are convicted, and sent to prison, the chance that they will be rehabilitated is minimal because of the influence of the prison environment.

Pretrial diversion, then, offers a two-fold advantage for police. First, consensual diversion may well adjudicate offenders who might beat the charges and make it back to the street. Second, if the diversion proves to be a positive experience, the person should be reinforcing desirable habits and forming better relationships. This is the opposite of prison life, where criminal behavior, brute force and dominance are reinforced. Either way, the police and society stand to come out ahead.

Undercover Law Enforcement and Cults

As the number and type of police undercover operations grow, officers are encountering a host of new hazards. This is especially true in narcotics law enforcement which is increasingly characterized by extremely dangerous, no-holds-barred, criminals.

There is nothing clean, sportsmanlike, or honorable about the narcotics scene, anywhere. It is a world of sleazy people dealing for high stakes, who face incredibly heavy penal sanctions should they be caught and convicted. Dopers are violent and gunfire is likely during drug arrests, as suspects often have access to an impressive array of weapons, many of them military and automatic, capable of immense firepower. Moreover, police drug investigations seem to involve more and more immigrants from Central and South America where, for some residents, drugs and violence have become a way of life. Police must assume that those detained or stopped for drug crimes may shoot first and ask questions later, for they have little to lose.

What this means to police, in undercover narcotics roles, is that the uncertainties accompanying such work are immense, even though almost every operation features several officers, in differing roles, working closely together. Some of the most sophisticated communications technology available is used by police but, in spite of concerted efforts to make undercover police operations safer, there are invariably casualties. Greater attention must be focused on assuring officer safety in undercover roles.

As in other types of police transactions, carelessness continues to plague undercover cops. For example, there are still officers wounded or killed, while serving search or arrest warrants, when desperate suspects inside houses or buildings fire shots blindly through doors. Officers, irrespective of role or assignment, should never stand in front of doorways!

It is almost standard procedure to put hidden transmitters on undercover officers who are infiltrating or dealing with narcotics or vice suspects. There are many hazards in doing so, but on balance, the transmitters are more likely to contribute to, rather than detract from, an officer's safety. However, in planning undercover operations which include body transmitters, contingency plans must be made to assure a prompt response and rescue should the bug be discovered. The plan, of course, will require having cover personnel nearby and may, also, include a diversionary act. Whatever the rescue scheme, all officers must be briefed on it in advance, and it is imperative that they instantly recognize that an emergency plan has been activated.

Misidentity of Officers by Other Officers

Accidental armed confrontations, between uniformed police and unidentified undercover officers, must be avoided at all costs during covert operations, raids, and warrant executions. Therefore, determining how a plainclothes or undercover officer can be readily identified by other police is an urgent problem, as personnel run a special risk of being mistaken for criminals.

Can a plainclothes officer on a deeply covert operation perform his or her mission with anonymity in the eyes of the public, yet be identifiable as an officer to other police? Realistically, the answer is negative. For that reason, every year, hundreds of officers face the harrowing prospect that they will find themselves in a life-threatening situation, and other police won't realize they are working for the same side.

There is no standard means by which an undercover officer may, with certainty and immediately, in a time of crisis, identify him or herself as law enforcement, without blowing all the preparation that has gone into setting up the operation. Additionally, not every force has devised a procedure for making such an identification, and those that did have found that contingency plans do not work with certainty. As a result, forces which have devised a means to prevent the misidentification of officers, have implemented the procedure only in particular cases. The procedure includes special measures which go into effect during narcotics deals in which covert officers must be protected, other types of raids, and during Presidential visits.

The most common procedure has plainclothes personnel wearing some unique, but unobtrusive, pin, badge, garment, sweatband, cap, etc. Sometimes a specific verbal command or password is used, followed by a precise, predetermined response. The utility of such a procedure is speculative, but some formal procedure appears better than none, considering the grave hazards undercover police face when mistakenly identified.

Many forces issue raid jackets to personnel who are working in civilian clothing, but serving on raid squads. The jackets, uniformly colored and plainly marked with the word POLICE or the name or initials of a specific agency, are intended to enable the quick identification of lawmen during operations.

A cardinal rule, with regard to officer safety in covert circumstances, is that the burden of providing a quick "I.D." always rests with the officer being challenged. This person must immediately convey his or her identity to uniformed personnel, as best can be done, even unconventionally if need be. Hopefully, however, the means of conveying one's identity will follow the exact procedure set out in the pre-incident briefing.

Drug Labs and Toxic Chemicals

Illicit drug operations, many of them global in scope, are making the world a smaller place. A drug lab, busted by the RCMP near the border in lower British Columbia in 1996, was one of the most sophisticated illegal labs ever discovered, manufacturing the designer drugs ecstasy (MDMA) and LSD for distribution in the U.S. and Europe. Communications between the labs and buyers were exchanged over high tech equipment which featured coded E-mail on the Internet.

Such operations pose a plethora of risks for police. Illicit drug labs frequently contain extremely dangerous chemicals, haphazardly stored, requiring entry teams to don protective clothing, isolation suits, and breathing gear. These labs are so toxic that in 1996, more than 40 dwellings in the state of Washington, which had been used for making methamphetamines, had to be condemned by the Washington State Department of Ecology. An unsuspecting, biologically and chemically unprotected entry team, walking into a meth house, could face severe and long-term health problems.

Not only are the chemicals themselves a grave danger, but cunning criminals have been known to booby-trap labs with explosive devices, conceal venomous snakes with their drug stashes, or emulate a popular Hollywood scene: tether, or allow to run free on the premises, ill-treated and vicious dogs, usually pit bulls or rottweilers.

How does law enforcement deal with such threats? The Royal Canadian Mounted Police has extensive background in this type of tactical operation. If they suspect explosives, the area is first cleared by a bomb dog and explosives team, before bringing in the drug section officers and a drug-sniffing canine. To protect against venomous snakes, officers should look for clues which suggest this type of booby-trap. If police find mice in a cage, which are live food for snakes, officers proceed with caution. The room entry team may carry carbon dioxide fire extinguishers with which to cool off any angry reptiles. The difficulty of getting past vicious dogs, unless they attack first and must be shot, is usually left to the K-9 officers.

Countersurveillance

Sometimes police themselves are targets of countersurveillance, set up by sophisticated gangs making huge profits from illegal drugs, gambling, burglary or robbery. Such measures, by high tech and ruthless gangs, make police work even more dangerous, raising the stress level of law enforcement personnel.

A variety of weapons and gadgetry are used by those engaged in countersurveillance. Electronics gear of all sorts is foremost among the hardware. An array of vehicles, including vans, recreational vehicles, and mobile homes, is likely to be used, as are aircraft and boats. A choice is made, based on the nature of the countersurveillance and the location of the transaction. Trained vicious dogs, used primarily to guard drug houses and surrounding property, may be part of a gang's countersurveillance package.

When signs of countersurveillance are detected and confirmed, police must anticipate that seasoned, professional crooks are at work. It is time to take a step backward and assess what is known of the suspects and to determine what, if any, additional personnel and equipment should be brought to bear on the case. Countersurveillance activities are the early warning signs that a police undercover operation may be in real jeopardy.

Administrators must be certain that undercover police, and those whose mission it is to protect the covert personnel, are fully trained to detect warning signs that criminals are engaging in counter-surveillance. One safeguard is to assemble as much intelligence as possible about the gang or organization being investigated, then analyzing that information to try to predict how the suspects may react to differing circumstances. It is crucial to carefully plan warrant services and high-risk arrests, as well as to anticipate and plan for the most likely eventualities which could spin off from an operation. Undercover work is by no means just another day at the office: it features contacts, often one-on-one, with people who are vicious, conniving, skeptical and engaged in illegal million dollar deals. In short, a small mistake can prove fatal.

Dealing with Cults and Urban Guerrillas

There seem to be more cults than ever before in American society. In fact, nationwide, a number of groups, whose membership espouses violence and elitist status separate from the mainstream of society, have been in confrontations with lawmen. These groups feature an anti establishment, anti-police mentality. Many of them are quick to resort to violence to preserve what they construe as their First Amendment rights. A few well-publicized groups of this nature include: the Branch Dividians of Waco, Texas fame; MOVE in Philadelphia where some 80 homes were incinerated when police closed in on them in May, 1985; and a pseudo religious cult in Memphis which took two officers hostage and tortured one, killing him.

These anti-social cults are far outside the mainstream of American life. Whether organized and motivated by political, supremacist, sexual, religious, or environmental beliefs, cults are of concern to police, since the time may come when law enforcement will have to deal with them. Accordingly, police must endeavor to secure intelligence about the groups, their membership, mission, philosophy, and armaments. The dynamics of cults should be identified, analyzed, and evaluated with regard to the planning of subsequent contacts and strategies. Officers must realize that they may be targeted by cultists merely because police represent the government. By appreciating these elements of cultism, officers enhance their prospects of staying alive.

Should an encounter appear to be inevitable, there is a paramount need to anticipate the degree of violence and property damage which may accompany a confrontation. Of course, the need to anticipate short-range political and media implications is urgent, too. When trouble is on the horizon, planning and earlier intelligence gathering assume gargantuan proportions. Handle with care, but with a plan, should be the hallmark of these operations. With luck, and unfortunately it does play a role when dealing with zealots, law enforcement can control such groups and minimize casualties among both officers and cultists.

Urban guerrillas, terrorists, and militias are not unlike the cultists. These are persons, and groups, who for reasons of revolution, community disruption, political extremism, and hatred of American institutions, use violence of all sorts to create panic. Arson, firebombings, explosive devices, and ambushes or snipings are only some of the means used by terrorists to rip at the fabric of society. These people reject American law, institutions, and democratic principles as they seek to intimidate people for whatever selfish purpose motivates them.

One of the most visible groups in this category has to be the Freemen, whose 81-day stand-off with the FBI, near Jordan, Montana, was a major media event in the spring of 1996.

Supremacist and militia groups, intent on disrupting government, have started stockpiling supplies in foreign venues. In the fall of 1996, in western Canada, the RCMP unearthed a huge cache of food, camping and survival gear, along with ammunition and shotguns, rifles, chemical suits and anti-tear gas masks. These items were traced to a militia group based in the United States.

The Importance of Intelligence

Elitist groups are a danger to police and society as a whole. One of the best ways to assure officer safety when dealing with them is through carefully gathered intelligence, surveillance, and undercover information. And, ideally, police agencies, locally, statewide, nationally, and internationally, should cooperate with one another in sharing information and educating officers about these dangers. Officers are much safer when they have some idea as to what risks they are facing. Planning and widespread solicitations for public cooperation will pay off when dealing with fringe groups, too.

O'er Amber Waves of Pot

Each year, from August to October, the "fall follies" take place in some parts of the United States. This is the time when police descend upon illicit cash crops of marijuana which are cultivated by growers for huge profits. In some locales the pot harvest is so big it is considered the mainstay of the local economy! Lawlessness is often a partner when an illicit enterprise assumes such stature. Therefore, police and others who seek to disrupt "business as usual" are often in danger.

It didn't take long for American police to begin identifying and raiding major pot fields, as soon as it became public knowledge that pot growing had blossomed into a multimillion dollar business. And it didn't take long for the pot growers to turn to violence. Homemade booby traps, featuring explosives and shotgun shells, lodged in steel or iron devices with trip wires, were found in one Oklahoma field, as were fishhooks hung head- or chest-high in overgrown cutting areas.

Another pot grower had imbedded punji spikes in his fields, while yet another had cut the rattles off of rattlesnakes and tied the deadly reptiles to marijuana plants. To these dangers, add the prospect that assault rifles and other deadly weapons may be used to ambush lawmen as they take part in drug raids.

On the legal front, prosecutors are often charging landowners and growers with tax law violations, rather than pursuing the relatively lax laws regulating the cultivation of marijuana. Some jurisdictions invoke asset forfeiture laws, which are the legal means by which the government may seize vehicles, equipment, cash and real estate if such assets were acquired with the proceeds of illegal drug deals. These kinds of pressures are essential weapons in the battle against pot farmers and other illicit drug traffickers.

Vans, Recreational Vehicles and Motor Homes

Vans, recreational vehicles, and motor homes are present on America's streets and highways in increasingly greater numbers. While, at one time, most of these vehicles were owned by 45 to 70 year-old couples, this is no longer so. Younger professional people with kids are choosing to own vans and RVs rather than buying luxury cars. And a huge number of customized vans, RVs, and motor homes, with extraordinary furnishings and electronic paraphernalia, are on the road, serving millions of people, a few of whom are drug dealers.

What does this mean to police? It means, for one thing, greater danger during traffic stops, because there are very few tactical problems in law enforcement that present officers with so many unknown factors. Yet police must balance the need to protect themselves, while making traffic stops, with the need to tactfully and politely address traffic violators, the majority of whom are respectable citizens.

It is risky for an officer to approach a van, RV, or motor home, even when its occupants have been pulled over for a routine stop. The design of these vehicles impedes the officer's vision. Often he or she cannot see the occupants or the inside layout, or detect movement within. The problem is worsened immeasurably if the vehicle is customized with darkly tinted glass. And there are many possible exits from some of these vehicles, a variable which exacerbates the danger, as does the number of windows, the possibility of sun roofs and pop-up tops, trap doors, and pop-out windows. There are unlimited cubbyholes within vans, RVs, and motor homes, if the plan is to conceal a person to mount a surprise attack on an unwary officer.

Occupant control is crucial to officer safety during any vehicle stop. Being able to see a vehicle's occupants and their hands is the ideal circumstance. Hence, officers are working at a distinct disadvantage when they take on vans, RVs, or motor homes. Understandably, these types of vehicles are a nightmare for police.

The first tactical move when pulling over vans, RVs, or motor homes is to summon back-up assistance. Then the location for the stop should be carefully and deliberately selected. It should be a locale which favors the police, insofar as that is possible. Then the patrol cars must be properly positioned. Next, officers should be extraordinarily alert when approaching any of these over-sized vehicles, fully aware of the tactical dilemma from the outset. In order to better the odds, officers should park the police units farther back from the suspect vehicle, than would be done ordinarily. The additional distance affords officers more time during an approach to observe the scene and valuable time to react and retreat to the squad cars, if necessary. There is no rush to draw close to the suspect vehicle, hence entering the close range kill zone.

Officers may chose to be innovative when approaching these types of vehicles. After radioing headquarters with the standard information about the location and purpose of the stop, description, and license of the vehicle, one officer may opt to walk behind the squad car and approach the suspect vehicle from the right side, as a second officer stands back on the left side. If the lawman is alone, the squad's passenger door may even be opened and slammed to give the impression of a second officer. During the approach, officers may be able to take advantage of a sneak peek at the occupants by using the vehicle's side-mounted rearview mirrors. Of course, officers can issue instructions to the occupants by using the police car's outside loud speaker. Explanations or commands may buy time, while awaiting support personnel.

If the occupants are suspected of more than a mere traffic violation, it is wise to use tactics common to a felony stop. This calls for backup officers and the positioning of officers and units, as a show of force, to discourage resistance from the suspects. Of course, police must be mindful of fields of fire, not just from the suspects, but from other officers. Police must look out for innocent bystanders, too, including those driving by in other traffic lanes, or moving around the vehicles on a median or shoulder.

In summary, vans, RVs, and motor homes are a fact of police life and are here to stay. While most occupants are law abiding, a few will be sought for crimes. The hazardous nature of dealing with persons driving these oversized vehicles is well-established, and officers must take thoughtful measures to minimize the risks. Otherwise, many police will lose their lives unnecessarily.

Chapter 9

LEGISLATIVE COUNTERMEASURES

Crime control seems very closely linked with the prompt reporting of offenses, the early detection of offenders, their immediate arrest, a speedy trial, and their conviction, followed by no-nonsense sentencing. These are the elements of deterrence, causing suspects to sense the certainty that something unpleasant will happen, and soon, if they misbehave and are caught. Officer safety seems inextricably linked to these elements.

Legislative bodies are supposed to be responsive to public sentiment and reflect society's attitude on issues. Sometimes it works this way and sometimes it doesn't. In any event, these bodies can help make police safer if they take favorable action on certain measures. Specific proposals about stiffening gun laws, especially those which apply to handguns, making capital punishment a reality rather than a hollow folly, and mandating that there be an autopsy whenever an officer is murdered would be sensible to enact into law. Some states have done so, to some extent, as has the federal government. Other timely measures focus on motor vehicle license plates and the use of solar glass in cars. These laws indirectly affect police officer safety.

In November, 1994, the International Association of Chiefs of Police hosted an important summit which addressed the broadly-based issue of murder in America and what can be done to reduce the carnage. Fifty-five law enforcement authorities and scholars fashioned a package of proven, promising, and innovative strategies for reducing homicide. Of course, these included measures which, if implemented, would help protect police.

Among the panel's recommendations for legislative initiatives were laws which, if passed, would:

- Increase sanctions for gun-involved crimes, particularly robberies;
- Allow police to seize weapons during domestic violence calls;
- Prohibit gun ownership by stalkers and domestic violence offenders;
- Reorient the juvenile justice system to promote swift and sure intervention against career juvenile offenders;
- Allow police to photograph, fingerprint, and document criminal behavior of career juvenile offenders;
- Allow interagency and interstate sharing of juvenile information among police and other agencies; and
- Raise the minimum drinking age, increase state or central control of alcohol sales, and limit prevalence of liquor stores through stringent store/population ratios.

The creative work of the IACP's Violence in America Summit was conducted by four panels, each focusing on one of the following murder/violence types:

- Youth violence and homicide;
- Confrontational violence and homicide;
- Robbery-related violence and homicide; and
- Intimate violence and homicide.

Each panel was asked to address the following three dimensions of its type of murder: (1) the extent and nature of the problem; (2) the current law enforcement response; and (3) strategies to address the problem. Not surprisingly, each panel declared that guns and drugs, including alcohol, typically appear as aggravating factors in murder and violence situations. The action agenda produced by the summit, in addition to the legislative proposals summarized above, included initiatives which law enforcement figures, community and government agencies, and persons in education and training roles could take.

Legislative bodies do not always act favorably on measures which could relate to officer safety. For example, at one time the United States Congress was asked to make attacks on police, firefighters, and judicial officers a federal offense. Hearings were held, but they proved inconclusive. The evidence presented was not sufficiently persuasive to cause the U.S. Senate to pass a bill of this nature, even though a similar statute exists with the National Bank Robbery Act and the respective states' robbery statutes. If a measure like that proposed had been passed, it may have been helpful to reducing attacks on officers.

On the other hand, there have been occasions when the U.S. Congress and states have passed measures which help streamline the criminal justice system and by so doing have better protected police. One such act sought to process accused criminals more quickly and efficiently through the system without impairing their constitutional rights. This was the federal Speedy Trial Act which called for a gradual reduction in the time between arrest and trial. Speedy trial acts, which most states have enacted, are believed to help make police safer because they take delay out of the system and set a get-to-trial time limit for all felony cases.

Set out below is a discussion about some specific sectors where legislation could be significant to reducing assaults on police.

Firearms Control Legislation

Firearms control legislation is seldom far removed from the public eye. It regularly resurfaces after the shooting of a prominent American. And it surely is among the most contentious, hotly debated, and emotional of America's domestic public safety issues. Gun control is, also, one of the most misunderstood issues.

Public opinion polls consistently indicate that over two of every three Americans feel that the easy availability of handguns "contributes a lot" to violence, and there should be tighter legislative reins over handgun sales with mandatory handgun registration. Yet, when such legislation pends in either the United States Congress or in state capitols across America, the most mail comes from those who oppose gun control. Public opinion and pro-gun control lobbyists all agree that steps should be taken to curb crime, but many Americans disagree, and often heatedly, as to whether a crackdown on gun sales and comprehensive gun registration would be an effective deterrent.

The all-time leading American spokesman for rigid firearms control legislation was J. Edgar Hoover, the venerable late director of the FBI. Consistently and unstintingly, he was committed to the most stringent controls. In September, 1967, he wrote pointedly in *The FBI Law Enforcement Bulletin* that:

> There is no doubt in my mind that the easy accessibility of firearms is responsible for many killings, both impulse and premeditated. The statistics are grim and realistic. Strong measures must be taken, and promptly, to protect the public.

Hoover called firearms seven times more lethal than other murder weapons. His point is underscored by the fact that, of the 2,852 lawmen murdered from 1960 to 1994, 2,667 (or 93.5 percent) were victims of firearms. Handguns, in contrast to long guns, took 2,021 (or almost 71 percent) of the officers' lives.

The correlation between the ready availability of handguns and assaults and murders of police officers should be of urgent concern to the authorities. There is a strong indication that one meaningful long-range measure which the United States Congress could take to reduce assaults on police, is the passage of effective federal handgun controls. Ideally, the stiff measures should be implemented by the states as well.

Historically, the first state regulation controlling the purchase and possession of firearms is found in the controversial Sullivan Law in New York State, enacted in 1911. The traditional objection to this type of regulation is the usual one raised against all firearm legislation: it burdens the law-abiding citizen, while failing to keep pistols out of the hands of criminals. The argument goes that criminals will not obey the law, but will steal, or even make a firearm. Proponents of this form of gun control do not dispute this, but point out that one benefit derived from a stiff Sullivan-type law is that it provides a basis for easily convicting gun-toting criminals. This is true, even where there is insufficient evidence to prove guilt beyond a reasonable doubt for a major offense such as murder, aggravated assault or robbery. Proving that a gunman merely possessed a firearm, without a license, is straight-forward compared to proving that he or she participated in a major crime.

Gun registration is not to be confused with gun confiscation, though it frequently is misunderstood as such. Registration is merely a matter of recording to whom each firearm rightfully belongs which establishes accountability, as has been done for decades with automobiles. To suggest that registering firearms, certainly all handguns, equates with or will lead to confiscation, is illogical. It would be like declaring that a law to keep unsafe cars off city streets will result in the confiscation of all autos. But as long as easily concealed handguns continue to exact their lethal toll of police, departments should take strong stands supporting handgun registration.

In the long run, it is apparent to many groups that stricter gun control measures, including handgun registration, are needed. Handgun registration infringes on no one's right to keep and bear arms. It might, however, sharply reduce a potential police killer's ability to murder. Registration may, in and of itself, prove to be insufficient, too, but until political leaders acknowledge that handguns are killing more Americans than they are protecting, it will suffice as a stopgap measure. Perhaps, someday, more meaningful legislation can be enacted. But, a start must be made at some level.

Almost every major advisory commission on crime since 1966 has advocated strong firearms control measures as one way to make life in the United States safer. None suggested that such legislation, if adopted, would bring about a change in the firearms picture overnight. Rather, measures along the lines that former FBI Director Hoover ardently supported, are really long-range in impact, benefitting our grandchildren.

The staggering percentage of criminal homicides perpetrated against police by firearms indicates that one form of gun restraint is warranted, if not long overdue. This is legislation which applies to handguns, leaving long guns out of the issue. There was movement in this area, on the national level, when the firearms provisions of the Omnibus Crime Control and Safe Streets Act and the Gun Control Act of 1968 were passed. This was the first important federal effort to curb the proliferation of weapons in America since 1934, when the National Firearms Act imposed a ban on ownership of submachine guns, then widely used in mob gang wars.

Although widely ballyhooed at the time of passage, the 1968 legislative provisions merely slowed the booming mail-order gun business, through which Lee Harvey Oswald bought the Italian army surplus rifle used to murder President John F. Kennedy in November, 1963. Yet the legislation, intended to curb the massive trade in cheap pistols called "Saturday night specials," contained a loophole. The measure banned the complete pistols, but allowed the import of parts. Of no surprise, the parts were imported and the cheap handguns were assembled domestically. The failure of this legislation was obvious: during the first four years of the new gun control laws, 1969 through 1972, imports of parts for cheap, pot metal street guns were sufficient to see the production of more than 4 million "Saturday night specials."

There has been strong rhetoric but not much significant legislation on the gun control scene, since 1968. A major disappointment for police came in 1984 when a bill to ban armor-piercing ammunition, which had been ricocheting around Congress for several years, was not enacted. That year the bill, banning cop-killer bullets, was lobbied to death by gun interests, fearing that if such a measure succeeded it may be the beginning of major firearms control legislation. If it had passed, the measure would have sensibly banned the manufacture, importation, and sale of armor-piercing bullets, which have been fired on police officers. Alarmingly, this ammunition is capable of piercing the protective vests worn by police.

Congress finally enacted a law meaningful to public safety in 1993 when the Brady Handgun Violence Prevention Act was passed, becoming effective on February 28, 1994. The Brady Act mandated, among other things, that there be a process to assure that people, applying to purchase handguns, would undergo background checks, often with an accompanying waiting period. The law left it to each state to determine whether to adopt a waiting period or some other clearance mechanism.

The Brady Act is seen as more of a deterrent than a prosecutive mechanism. Its purpose is to keep firearms out of the hands of illegal drug users, convicted felons, fugitives from justice, and mentally ill persons. Brady did not impose any reporting requirements on gun dealers or law enforcement officials, so neither comprehensive nor national data on handgun purchase applications and denials are available.

Although national data are lacking, the Bureau of Justice Statistics (BJS) conducted a study to provide an overview of how the deterrent procedures work in various states, to help measure the impact of the Brady Act. The BJS reports that in 18 states, as of January, 1996, 2,229,430 applications to purchase a firearm had been processed. Of these, 45,369 were rejected, a rate of just over two rejections for every hundred applications. An unanticipated benefit was that several of the people, whose applications were rejected, were easily located and taken in to custody for outstanding warrants and other offenses not directly related to the handgun purchase application.

Another measure, signed by the President in late 1994, required that any ammunition magazine, produced for a handgun, could have a capacity of no greater than ten rounds. This measure, in an oblique fashion, addressed the assault weapons issue. What was not foreseen by politicians and gun control advocates was that the firearms manufacturing industry would make big money by developing, producing, and marketing a new generation of purse and pocket pistols. Many women purchased these ultracompact handguns, with magazines of six to ten rounds, to have a means of protecting themselves with an easily concealed lethal weapon. These weapons are proving to have maximum stopping power.

It is too soon to know what, if any, impact this new class of handgun will have on assaults on police. Likewise, it is not yet possible to gauge the impact of the growing number of states, 31 in 1996, which have passed conceal-and-carry laws giving law-abiding citizens the right to bear concealed weapons.

In spite of the passage of the Gun Control Act of 1968 and the Brady Act, as well as the development of ultracompact weapons and the newer conceal-and-carry laws, the handgun debate goes on and on. In the meantime, the most realistic short-term solution appears to be for local police to strictly enforce all gun control laws enacted in their state, including background checks, registration, waiting periods, and other licensing prerequisites, before a person may purchase a handgun.

Another helpful measure would be for states that have not yet done so, to pass mandatory prison sentencing laws for conviction of serious crimes, including those in which the use of real or simulated firearms played a prominent role. Mandatory minimum sentences would be longer if the accused had previously been convicted of a crime involving a firearm.

In conclusion, there is irony in the gun control squabble of a sadly humorous sort. President Reagan always opposed federal handgun legislation, and in 1983 he reiterated his position to 4,000 cheering National Rifle Association members. The irony is that those, who attended that speech, had to walk past metal detectors to hear the President, who had been the victim of a violent attack by an unstable man with easy access to a handgun, early in his administration.

Capital Punishment

Legislative provisions for capital punishment in the United States date back toward the founding of the nation. One of the earliest provisions was set out in Section 19 of The Mint Act of April 2, 1792 which was designed to protect United States coinage at the U.S. Mint at Philadelphia. Death was the penalty should one be convicted of embezzlement or the intentional debasement of gold or silver with fraudulent intent. Interestingly, the State of Pennsylvania's statute called for a fine and imprisonment for the same offenses! Such convolutions in penalties have characterized the long road of capital punishment in America over the years.

Capital punishment, as a sanction, rocked along for almost 200 years until it came to a de facto moratorium from 1967 to 1977 as the nation awaited a United States Supreme Court decision on the issue. The judgment was rendered in 1972 in the *Furman vs. Georgia* case which, in essence, invalidated death penalty statutes, as then administered, on the basis that death sentences were "freakishly" and arbitrarily imposed. *Furman* effectively caused those states which wanted the capital penalty to draft around the issues which had brought capital punishment to a standstill. The High Court revived capital punishment in 1976 when it found in the *Gregg vs. Georgia* case that various state capital punishment laws passed since *Furman* sufficiently reduced the randomness permitted by the earlier statutes.

The alleged merits of capital punishment are linked with several familiar arguments: it acts as a deterrent to murder; prevents future heinous crimes from being committed; and serves the retributive side of justice. Add to this the fact that when kidnapping had reached epidemic proportion in the mid-1930s and was made punishable by death, kidnapping disappeared almost at once. It is also argued that the number of murders across America would go down if the number of legal executions went up, if a death sentence in fact meant death.

These considerations, be they real or imagined, weigh heavily on the minds of police. Capital punishment also seems to serve police and the public as a morale booster. Indeed, many officers feel their lives will be endangered if capital punishment is eliminated by judicial fiat. Officers also feel their lives to be endangered if states that have capital punishment do not execute condemned killers.

Whether the arguments propounded for capital punishment or officers' fears are scientifically valid or not, is another matter. It needs to be recognized, regardless of how little proof is available for retention of capital punishment, that law enforcement personnel favor it highly.

Analyzing the subtleties of intent in the mind of a cop-killer is a difficult task. It is hard to say that an officer's life could have been saved had capital punishment been in effect at the time of an incident. No one, other than the suspect himself, really knows for sure whether the threat of execution would have caused him or her to avert the act.

One offshoot of capital punishment may work against its real or imagined deterrent value. It seems that capital punishment prolongs court proceedings because of the certainty that if convicted, the condemned person, through counsel, will pursue every available avenue of appeal to reverse the death sentence. In Oklahoma, as in all but one of the 38 states that have a capital punishment statute, death sentence convictions are automatically referred to the Court of Criminal Appeals for review, a process which up to 1995 took five or more years in several instances.

Another offshoot is that if the possible punishment may be death, that juries will be reluctant to impose it. The added weight that the question of life or death imposes on jury deliberations is sometimes thought to prompt acquittal or a finding of a less severe degree of homicide. This spirit may have been at work in Oklahoma, for of the 81 suspects in the 59 Oklahoma police murder incidents, only two were actually executed, although eight sentences of death were handed down. If these contentions are true in death-penalty states, then these are strong considerations to be analyzed in the debate over capital punishment. If punishment is uncertain, even with the death penalty on the books, the deterrent effect seems compromised.

Arguments whirl, pro and con, about capital punishment. Yet morale and the deterrent effect are the major factors which police officers see as favoring capital punishment. It follows that as long as police are fired upon and officers continue to be murdered in the line of duty, these two factors should be acknowledged as substantial rationale when legislators deliberate the passage of capital punishment statutes.

From 1977 through 1994, only 256 men and one woman had been executed in the United States. Texas, Florida, Virginia, Louisiana, and Georgia accounted for just over 70 percent of these. On the other end of these data, 13 of the 38 capital punishment states put no one to death during these 18 years, which sharply questions whether capital punishment means anything, being just a big, phony paper tiger. Realistically, a law is not really a law when it is not used, as in these 13 states.

In conclusion, here are some interesting figures. Over the 18 years, 1977 - 1994, there were 351,351 homicides in America. During this same time, only 257 persons were executed, an average of but one murderer for every 1,367 murder victims. Since 1983, the pace of executions has quickened across America, though it has not become a groundswell. But the accelerated pace has come at a time when public support for carrying out the death penalty hovers at about the 77 percent approval mark, virtually a 40-year high. Police officers hope the time will soon come when executions are no longer front-page news, for police will see that as justice served.

Assuring That There Is an Autopsy

An autopsy, a post-mortem medical examination of a body, can also be classified as a procedure that may save police lives. Its value is that a qualified pathologist can almost always establish a person's cause of death through standard medical practices. The facts will not only help an investigation and prosecution, but are invaluable for research into police deaths. Mandating that there be an autopsy every time a police officer is killed in the line of duty would help assure a complete accounting of what happened.

During the Oklahoma police murders research project, the official autopsy report in one case began, "The body is that of an adult, unembalmed white male that measures 191 cm. (75") in length, and weighs approximately 80 kgs., (175 lbs.). The body is naked. There is complete rigor mortis and the body temperature is cool." The officer was, the report went on, ". . . the victim of a gunfire incident which occurred . . . during application of a District Court Search Warrant for narcotics and dangerous drugs at the described residence."

As unemotional, clinical, precise and scientific as the autopsy report may be, the importance of it in this case was found in the last entry. That entry, labeled "Final Impression of the Cause of Death," provided the district attorney with the basis for convicting the suspect in this incident. The state, backed by medical facts, could set out the specific cause of death, leaving that fact virtually immune from defense inferences that death may not have been actually perpetrated by the defendant.

Autopsy surgery is one of the oldest procedures in medical science. Its purpose is to meet the need for detailed diagnosis of the cause of death. Moreover, it is an important procedure since as many as one-fourth of the determinations of cause of death made at the scene by physicians and police may be inaccurate. Clearly, there is a reason for performing an autopsy, and it is not idle medical curiosity, as many people believe.

Adequate medicolegal investigation is absolutely essential to law enforcement and the prosecution of crime. It answers such crucial questions as: (1) what was the exact cause of death? (2) was death caused by one, two, or more gunshot wounds, etc., a blunt instrument, asphyxiation, or a fall? and (3) was the obvious trauma really the cause of death? Other urgent questions, too, should be resolved by autopsy when a police officer is an apparent murder victim, for the case may become embroiled in a hotly contested criminal trial. Also, an analysis of post mortem findings may help police training officers identify preventive measures that can be taken to protect officers from homicidal assaults.

Many states have embraced the state medical examiner system, replacing the creaking, antiquated county coroner system. The coroner system was developed by English knights who served the Crown hundreds of years ago. A modern state medical examiner law requires all deaths known or suspected to have resulted from accident, suicide, or homicide to be subject to the jurisdiction of the state medical examiner, a qualified pathologist. This is true regardless of the period of survival following the injury and whether there was medical attendance during time of the survival.

In Oklahoma, such a law has been in effect since 1962. From 1910 through 1961 state law called for local justices of the peace to perform the functions of the coroner. There was no requirement that justices or coroner's jury members possess medical knowledge or investigative skills. Moreover, justices of the peace serving as coroners were not required to hold inquests in every case of violent death. Discretion in such matters was a characteristic of the system.

Fortunately, an autopsy is becoming a normal procedure when lawmen are murdered in many states, a product of medical examiners laws. Moreover, the incidence of autopsies in remote areas of states where facilities for autopsy are less than ideal, is evidence that the medical examiner law is working where it has become law.

In conclusion, the rapidly changing character of American society adds a new urgency to the importance of a detailed post mortem medical diagnosis. Moreover, the importance of competent medico-legal investigations of death is not linked merely to trial testimony. It is necessary to take the speculation out of the cause of death in an era of national violence and suspicion of government and its agents. The procedure is essential to the resolution of civil suits, too, especially those which may be linked with litigation over worker's compensation and life insurance settlements. It is especially relevant where double indemnity payment may be an issue.

Mandating License Plate Improvements

To most people, an automobile license plate and the number it bears has no meaning at all. But to police officers a license plate number can be related to life or death! How is this? It's simple: A license number is the most direct means to identifying who owns a vehicle, who may be in it, or who should *not* be in it!

Surprisingly, officers make about as many motor vehicle identifications from the *front* license plate as from those which are rear-mounted. This, of course, assumes than an automobile bears a front mounted plate, which is *not* the case in about 20 of the 50 United States and in nine of Canada's 12 provinces and territories.

Front- and rear-mounted license plates are important to police because these are directly related to officer safety. In short, a license plate number, checked through the computer, may render a crucial tip-off that there is something amiss about a vehicle or that its occupants are wanted.

Most police patrolling is on two-way streets, whether in towns, cities, or country roads. This means that officers will see at least as many, if not more, *front*-mounted than rear-mounted plates, because police on patrol most often meet vehicles on the roadway, rather than overtake them.

Weather is another consideration which bears on the relevance of front- and rear-mounted license plates to police safety. Snowfall often covers the rear of parked vehicles, leaving the front plate as the most ready means for an officer to check an automobile, assuming the state requires a front plate.

It is true that virtually all traffic stops which police make for hazardous moving violations involve approaching the vehicle and driver, and passengers, from the rear. Also, almost all forces require that the arresting officer radio notice of the car's make and license number to the dispatch center or make an instant computer query about the vehicle from within the patrol unit. In any event, a check is made against the stolen car list. It is proper that this entire procedure occur before an officer in the patrol car contacts a motorist who has been pulled over.

The routine nature of traffic stops should not obscure the reason why front-mounted plates are important to officer safety. There are a host of reasons other than traffic stops that make it necessary for officers to interview persons in autos or to approach unoccupied cars. These include occasions when police approach cars which appear disabled or abandoned, or when persons in autos appear intoxicated or under the influence of other drugs. In addition, officers may perceive that one or more occupants may be sick, asleep, or showing unruly behavior. And there are occasions when occupants seem to the officer as acting furtively, as if engaging in some suspicious activity or stashing something out of the officer's sight. These are anxious times for police, and it is to an officer's advantage to know as much as possible at once about the auto and its occupants. Information stemming from a plate number checked through dispatch or by means of the in-car computer can dictate how an officer is going to respond.

There are also instances when officers on patrol are struck by a combination of circumstances which naggingly tell them the vehicle and its occupants warrant closer scrutiny, for reasons not yet known, or which may turn out to be none at all. Officers sometimes must make their approach from in front of the auto in question, or from an angle, as from a sidewalk or in a parking lot. Under such circumstances, it is urgent that police can read a license number and check it before committing to a contact with the driver.

Passenger vehicle license plates and annual validation stickers should be reflectorized, too, for the same reasons there should be a front plate, which is visibility. Legislative bodies have done a much better job on mandating reflectorization: in 1995, only a few states did not oblige that their license plates and validation stickers be reflectorized to enhance night identification by police.

That assaults and officer injuries could have been prevented if there had been a front license plate, which was also reflectorized, on a suspect vehicle is speculative. However, just about every officer can cite several instances when he or she was at serious risk for want of a front plate for early identification.

It is timely that there be legislation across the United States and Canada requiring that every motor vehicle bear a front and rear reflectorized license plate. The International Association of Chiefs of Police has passed a resolution strongly supporting such a measure, pointing out that this is a small, inexpensive measure that can mean a great deal to the safety of officers on patrol, while aiding them in the performance of their duties. The actual cost of a pair of reflectorized license plates and validation stickers is very nominal and may be passed on to the motoring public at registration renewal time. This is a modest cost when compared with the toll in officer injuries and fatalities.

Nontransparent or Reflective Glass and Window Tinting

Modern technology and products stemming from space research have fostered many innovations to ease life and enhance comfort. For years, one product, nontransparent or highly solar reflective glass, has been used by the construction industry to enhance building appearance and reduce air conditioning costs. In the 1980s, the product was adapted for installation as motor vehicle glass. So used, a car's cab can be made nontransparent when viewed from the outside.

Whether auto glass is reflectorized or heavily tinted, police are alarmed and feel anxiety if they are unable to see what's going on inside the cab of a motor vehicle. Since police handle millions of cases each year involving motor vehicles, they feel strongly that vehicles with extremely tinted windows which preclude seeing inside vehicles under normal day or lighted conditions, constitute a grave danger. Rear window ornamental picture decals also dramatically reduce visibility from the outside, placing officers at a distinct disadvantage.

In practice, while the United States government regulates new-car equipment through its Federal Motor Vehicle Safety Standards (FMVSS), each state decides how dark windows can be. What occurs is that many states permit the installation of aftermarket window tinting which appears to circumvent FMVSS provisions, a circumstance very troublesome to police.

Police are not opposed to reasonable window tinting and the use of reflectorized glass, within sensible parameters, because there are solid reasons for using such materials in motor vehicles. The upshot is that the National Highway Safety Traffic Administration, working with all parties, should aim for uniformity across the nation. As authorities work with interested parties, including those who manufacture the materials, the concerns unique to the nation's police should not be forgotten. The Highway Safety Committee of the International Association of Chiefs of Police strongly recommends that action of the nature set out above be taken.

Chapter 10

OTHER THINGS CAN BE DONE

There are other casualty reduction possibilities which exceed proposals set out earlier. Their shaping and further development will help departments and individuals cope, long- and short-range, with the immensely complicated problem of attacks on police.

One of the most immediate measures that forces can take is to make certain that the public is informed about the dangers facing their police. Additionally, police forces should frankly confront the problems which alcohol and illegal drugs pose for officers, as well as the impact of television and media violence on street cops. While not a casualty reduction measure, police should assure that benefits afforded survivors are adequate in the event a life is lost.

Informing the Public of the Dangers Facing Police

American police officers are a key form of institutional authority, bearing important responsibilities, duties, powers, and prerogatives as society's enforcers of the law. They are the living embodiment of liberty within the framework of order. Yet the police, as the most visible symbols of government, come under sharp philosophical and personal attack from time to time. That physical assaults on police have occurred in alarming numbers and intensity since 1960 was shown in Table 1.1, in Chapter 1. Attacks remain a serious concern of considerable magnitude to the victims—police officers—who need public support *now*, more than ever.

"Support Your Local Police" is a phrase which can lead to more than support. If citizen energies are properly channeled, police lives may be saved. Citizen support for police is by no means a novel concept. Yet, the public must know what can be most useful to help, and then be encouraged to act.

Spreading information is vital, once the force has agreed to what it would like citizens to do to help. Patrol officers, especially, should be well-versed in the department's public involvement game plan. Moreover, all civilian and sworn police personnel must know the "hows" and "whys" of police work and excel in describing their work and needs to the public. The more citizens understand about the work of police, the easier it will be for the public to assist officers.

The police, themselves, must know about nonpolice community social service agencies which can help the public. For example, after a large western city established a mental health care center as one of its social service agencies, the police department distributed a one-page bulletin to all officers explaining the center's role and services, and who was entitled to use them. Officers were then able to spread the word to the people on the street who became aware that the mental health clinic could help them face their problems. Another example is for police to know about homes or centers where victims of spousal abuse may be referred for treatment and protection from their abusers. Such centers are helpful to police by reducing the prospect of family quarrels and preventing related stress situations. This helps police.

Dealing with Chemical Dependency

Tippling and recreational drug use, as portrayed on stage, in movies, and on television, loses a lot of its humor when casualties from alcohol and drug abuse are featured. Unfortunately, the nation's Number One mental health problem eludes resolution. The voices warning against alcohol and illegal drug ingestion seem drowned out by other causes, for few want to tangle with phantoms which affect so many of us, and our family members, in such embarrassing ways. It is doubly unfortunate that some police officers, like other members of society, have their own personal demons. Drug abuse, being illegal, is less common among police, but beer, wine, and mixed drinks are common social fare found in abundance at law enforcement gatherings.

Except as applies to alcohol consumption and drunken driving, Americans have yet to acknowledge the horrendous impact of excessive drinking and the use of illegal drugs on violent crime and loss of life. With the exception of reducing officer carelessness and complacency, there is no single front where a breakthrough could prove more meaningful in reducing assaults on police. The problem of chemical dependency is immense, touching many families and almost every area of life, yet it is shrugged off because there is a gigantic contradiction: alcohol use is not only legal, its consumption is socially acceptable as long as one's intake is viewed as not excessive. On the other hand, illegal drugs are not socially acceptable except among persons who defy the law and use them.

How immense is the problem? According to the United States Department of Health, Education and Welfare, the Congressional Office of Technology Assessment, and other sources, there are:

1. Some 95 million Americans who drink alcoholic beverages, of whom about one in every ten either is an alcoholic, being physically dependent on alcohol, or is an alcohol abuser, a person who drinks to excess;

2. Some 18,000 fatalities from auto crashes each year where alcohol was a factor, and several thousand more deaths where drugs other than alcohol contributed to the carnage;

3. Statistics which show that about one of every two homicides is alcohol-related;

4. About 150 *billion* dollars lost to U.S. industry each year because of alcohol or other substance abuse;

5. Thirteen percent of convicted offenders who committed crimes to obtain money with which to buy illegal drugs;

6. About 23 percent of inmates incarcerated because of illegal drug activities; and

7. Indications that chemical dependency among minority group members leads to blocked opportunities, inadequate medical care, unemployment, and poor school performance.

Of all chemical substances, **alcohol** is America's most abused drug and, at the same time, the most advertised and misrepresented. It is consistently presented by giant commercial enterprises as the nectar of good humor, assuring conviviality, sophistication, and popularity. Advertising suggests that alcohol solves problems, opens doors to business, social, and sexual success, while portraying the drinker as a mature, well-adjusted adult. In truth, alcohol abuse impacts society and police officers enormously in many, many ways.

Police see no humor, conviviality, maturity, or sophistication when a drink-crazed husband savagely beats his wife and kids, then wields a firearm, threatening to kill the first cop who attempts to "meddle in his business." Madison Avenue advertising firms, paid big bucks by the breweries and distillers, ignore the ugly side of alcohol.

Of the 61 officers murdered in the 59 Oklahoma incidents, preincident drinking by suspects was a salient factor in over 70 percent of the killings, which exceeds the alcohol factor in homicides generally. Any way you look at it, alcohol and drug use pose a giant headache which always spells trouble for police.

There are no surefire, exclusive measures which can suddenly free police from interacting with people who have been drinking. Prohibition, which was a symbol of hypocrisy and stiff-necked repression, didn't work in 1920s. Liquor laws have proven to be no solution, and their enforcement has been arbitrary. And it is disappointing that physicians, psychologists, and psychiatrists have been unable to discover any single treatment method that will invariably produce satisfactory results. In fact, if anything has emerged from decades and billions of dollars cast at this massive social problem, it is that no widespread, dramatic changes have been effected among Americans as a group, and problem drinkers and drug users specifically.

Despite limited success so far, there are compelling reasons for alcohol and drug rehabilitation specialists and organizations to continue to face the problem squarely and nurture programs which may prove useful. Several steps should be taken.

First, bosses need to get tougher on alcohol abuse and the use of controlled substances in public and private workplaces, including within police departments.

Second, the nation should continue to support long-range programs to discourage alcohol abuse, alcoholism and other drug abuse among young people. Education and a positive police presence in the schools, conducting programs such as Drug, Awareness, Resistance, Education (DARE) are important. Intensification of such programs is warranted.

Third, and there is movement along this front, there must be new methods for handling people who fall into police custody for drunkenness, without accompanying criminal misbehavior. Such means include, but are not limited to, the bootcamp approach for youthful offenders, and the decriminalization of drunkenness, then diverting problem drinkers and drug abusers into a variety of community alcohol and drug treatment programs. Another virtue to these approaches is that they make it easier for persons to overcome "denial," as it is more acceptable to suffer from a disease than a "personal weakness."

Fourth, alcoholism warrants treatment as an illness, not as a criminal offense, and there is progress toward public acceptance of this concept. The notion that alcohol is America's largest often untreated, yet treatable, illness is gaining backers from many quarters, including leading health professionals.

Fifth, the American attitude that alcohol and, to a lesser extent, controlled substances are essential as icebreakers at various fraternal, social, and business events must be changed.

Sixth, alcohol and common recreational **drugs** are drugs and must be identified and understood as such. People must realize that what they are drinking, or otherwise ingesting, will likely result in their experiencing lower inhibitions, slower than normal response times and perhaps increased aggression and foolish behavior. In short, when a person chooses to ingest chemical substances, that person, like it or not, accepts accompanying responsibilities of a very grave personal nature and will be held accountable for one's actions.

Seventh, there must be greater consideration afforded, and less social pressure put on, those who either do not drink at all, or use alcohol in moderation. Parental and peer group alcohol use has a great influence on others, especially the young and aspiring. A staggering drunk, telling his son about the evils of smoking dope, is not likely to make a very positive long-term impression on the youth.

Eighth, there are important measures that police organizations may take. A vigilant department looks for signs which suggest that certain officers may be suffering health problems, perhaps related to substance abuse. If such problems are identified and addressed, it is more likely that officers will be better able to stay alert on the street, without the disadvantages of fatigue, mental stress, or frayed tempers.

Police departments should make tactful, concerted efforts to identify and treat their problem drinkers. In doing so, supervisors should confine their remarks to job performance, noting in essence that "something isn't right here," and avoiding judgmental comments, while referring an officer to a health services provider for evaluation.

Remedial programs to help these employees may be established through county or state mental health officials, whose mission is to identify abusers, helping them recognize their problem, and make suitable referrals for assessment and treatment. This should be done while the officers are on the job. Larger forces may form Alcoholics Anonymous chapters or other support groups for the rehabilitation of their own members, along with force-wide education and counseling programs.

In summary, reducing alcohol and drug abuse would reduce violent crime, and prevent many accidental deaths and property damage. No one who understands human nature believes that human beings can be made temperate by repressive measures and legislation. Rather, the nation must try a combination of measures featuring intervention, pharmacological treatments, detoxification, psychotherapeutic and behavioral programs, education, legislation, and counseling, to name a few. Moreover, programs should be fashioned to meet individuals' needs, rather than trying to mold people into programs that do not take into account the clients' personal characteristics and needs.

The government's role should not be limited to underwriting programs and addiction counseling, but should include promoting the virtues of restraint. The surgeon general's strong anti-tobacco campaign and legislation banning smoking in restaurants, on commercial aircraft, and in office buildings are good examples of programs that seem to be working. Schools, educators, and coaches can play prominent roles, too, by setting good examples for students who may have no suitable role model at home. And there must be continuing, concerted research on the social, legal, and medical fronts as pertains to chemical dependency and societal responsibilities.

Television and Media Violence

What a paradox! People pack theaters to see films featuring violence at its worst, coldly and explicitly done. Then they head home to communities where crime rates are disturbing. Meanwhile, persons too fearful to go out at night rent home movies, or turn on television, and settle in to enjoy the evening's pillaging, fighting, shooting, and murder, safe behind deadbolted doors. In short, it's hard to find an evening of commercial television, cable media, or a rental video free from heavy violence, often of a very graphic and imaginative sort.

Violence portrayed by the entertainment industry probably triggers more attacks against police than will ever be documented. Often, cop-fighting is made to appear the norm, an acceptable, usual part of every police-suspect transaction. It has almost reached the point where any two-bit hoodlum feels compelled to fight, rather than to surrender peacefully, as many used to do. Waging a titanic fight for all to see, just like his fictional counterparts in everyday police thrillers, gives a thug identity among his pals. Police face great uncertainty as to how the action will go down when making arrests, especially if suspects must be taken from among their friends, or out of crowded public places. The influence of the media may be one reason.

Some say that violence is a fact of life and inherent in the nature of humans. These people see violence as an art form and favor depicting it as such, saying violence in media only mirrors violence in society. But, need it be portrayed so precisely and so graphically? Grisly scenes may well titillate the most latent desires of emotionally strained people who need only the blueprint for violence to induce them into acts of anti-social behavior.

Of little surprise, violence on television has been shown to encourage violent crime on the streets. This was one of the conclusions of the 1968 National Commission on the Causes and Prevention of Violence. It was reconfirmed in 1982 by a National Institute of Mental Health study which flatly stated that it found overwhelming evidence that excessive violence on television caused aggressive behavior in children. By 1996, there have been over 3,000 studies, about 85 of them original research, and all of them but one indicated a causal relationship between television violence and violence in real life. Researchers at the University of California at Santa Barbara, working jointly with those at the University of Wisconsin, found that extremely violent films resulted in desensitization to rape, murder, and assorted mayhem, reducing empathy for victims. Such a breakdown in values, the result of over exposure to violence, certainly becomes alarming when viewed beside a 1992 study by the American Psychological Association which estimated that the average child in the United States witnesses 100,000 acts of simulated violence before finishing grade school!

Violent behavior has escalated over the years, especially among youth from broken homes and poor families. These kids, and even those better off economically but lacking relationships of depth or meaning, often find their way into street gangs where they play out roles suggested by television, movies, and Gangsta rap music, using these crutches as substitutes for real life experiences. Without realizing it, kids are lulled into the delusion that television reflects real life, when in fact, it serves up primarily fantasy on a stage where there is no satisfactory demarcation line between reality and make-believe. It is small wonder that some teenagers use violence and gangs as a means for being recognized and establishing their own identity. For such disenchanted young people, violence is the pathway to big-shotism, cars, excitement, girls, dope, and cash. In 1993, Larry Bratt, a Maryland prison inmate serving life for murder, stated that many of these young gang-bangers were influenced by television:

> Every day America's 4,000 prisons and jails receive an influx of young African-American males and new inmates. Many of the million-plus inmates have been convicted of senseless crimes of violence. The majority of these young men first encounter crime and a glamorized view of the drug trade through a TV set.

Gang involvement nationwide is growing at an alarming rate. For example, in 1988 studies estimated that some 70,000 young people belonged to street gangs in Los Angeles. In 1996, police were estimating that upwards of 500,000 teens belong to more than 1,200 youth gangs in that city! One can only speculate about the impact which violence portrayed by television and other media have had on these young people and their street violence.

Several parent groups, most prominently the Parent Music Research Center (PMRC), led by Tipper Gore, wife of Vice-President Al Gore, and the Parent Teacher Association (PTA) believe that a relatively new phenomenon, gangsta rap and its videos, played over and over on MTV, lead to increased gang violence by promoting themes that degrade women, glorify drugs and gang activity, and deify violence against police. The hateful anti-police anthem, "Cop Killer" by Ice-T, which caused an outcry from law enforcement professionals across the land, is a prime example of this reckless and dangerous trend in the genre. Hardly ideal role models at their best, some gangsta rappers have actually seen the violent themes reflected in their music turn into reality. Snoop Doggy Dogg was charged in connection with a murder; Flavor Flav was once picked up for shooting at a man he suspected of having had sex with his girlfriend; and rapper Tupak Shakur was arrested for shooting two police officers in Atlanta a few years before he was fatally gunned down in Las Vegas in a 1996 shooting which police are yet to solve.

Beginning in the 1980s, and cascading into the tumultuous 1990s, some high-profile copycat crimes seem to have been inspired by the graphic violence portrayed in popular films. John Hinkley, Jr's, attempted assassination of President Reagan in 1981 appeared to have been inspired by the movie "Taxi Driver," in which a cab driver unsuccessfully tried to assassinate a presidential candidate. The press reported that Timothy McVeigh, charged in the 1995 Oklahoma City federal office building bombing, may have been influenced by "Blown Away," a film about a demented serial bomber. In "The Money Train," the audience saw a subway token collector set on fire. Three days after the movie was released, it really happened in Brooklyn! And one-half hour after watching the TV show "The Burning Bed," a man torched his estranged wife to death. Moreover, the film "Natural Born Killers," directed by Oliver Stone, sparked a controversial lawsuit after an unbalanced pair of movie watching sociopaths went on a copycat killing spree. "Serial Killa," by gangsta rapper Snoop Doggy Dogg, reportedly got a 16-year-old and his friends so worked up, that they stabbed to death his 80-year-old grandparents. In a second incident, in 1994, an eleven-year-old Ohio boy accidentally shot and killed his three-year-old sister and wounded an older sister while waving a gun around imitating Snoop Doggy Dogg.

The real impact of a constant diet of Hollywood style violence is a highly contentious issue with a host of social variables cast into the matrix. Consider all of the popular violent television programming that receives no scrutiny whatsoever. Very few small-screen events can attract a crowd around the television any quicker than a real life bone crushing brawl during the Super Bowl, or a stick-swinging fight during the Stanley Cup. Some noted roughhouse professional athletes, ironically called "policemen" in ice hockey, have not only become rich, but have gained public adulation by weaving a subtle mystique around their capacity for violence.

Television is a complex, big league communications device with great impact on public opinion. In our nation, the power of television is fully understood by savvy politicians. They know that they have to come across well in America's living rooms if elections are to be won. The visual media, especially television, is capable of such immense influence on human behavior and personalities that it would be naive to discount its influence on criminal behavior.

Measures to counter the excessive violence and gory escapist daydreams, characterizing some movies and television shows, are not easy to set out. Ideally, of course, viewers could turn off over-violent shows, stay away from the box office, and leave offensive CDs and cassettes on the shelves at the stores. Sponsors, too, could help by refusing to underwrite violent programs. Unfortunately, violence and the media constitute such a profitable commercial union that sponsors and financial backers are always available. So far, the Federal Communications Commission (FCC) has been ineffective at implementing any guidelines of consequence to root out excessive television or cable violence. Perhaps the FCC could have had more impact on program content and scheduling if the agency had taken a stronger position against violence during television's formative years, but that is water under the bridge.

Unless government rethinks priorities, the probability of assertive FCC action against TV violence seems unlikely in the 1990s. The federal agency has been a victim of severe budget cuts, office closings and forced employee layoffs. Historically, a strong stand by the FCC likely never took place because the politicians, who ultimately run the agency, feared that any attempt to impose censorship or program scheduling controls on the industry would result in a serious legal challenge over First Amendment rights. In what may be a prophetic glimpse into the future, recently the FCC issued a sterile statement informing the TV industry that it is expected to set up a system of guidelines to voluntarily regulate its own program content.

It appears that the most effective approach to curbing the violence so far has come from organized groups with specialized concerns, such as parents, clergy, police, and others. For example, Tipper Gore's group, PMRC and the PTA, succeeded in getting parental warning labels on offensive music and printed lyrics. Public and parental pressure, not the FCC, prompted many radio stations to remove the worst of gangsta rap from their play lists. And, in 1992, pressure from police organizations around the nation embarrassed Time Warner into dropping rap artist Ice-T, after the "Cop Killer" debacle. Then, three years later, Time Warner, unsettled by the negative publicity, sold off its share of Interscope Records, purveyors of gangsta rap.

There is a hopeful sign that government and the media may finally be getting serious about addressing the problem. Recently, the President and Congress both came out in support of V-chip computer technology which would allow parents to block out programs they find unsuitable for their children. Soon thereafter, President Clinton held a summit with Hollywood executives who agreed to come up with a TV ratings plan by January, 1997, similar to the G, PG, PG-13 and R ratings used for the past 28 years in the movie industry. Just who oversees the ratings is sure to be contentious, as there are early indications that the industry itself plans to do it. Critics are quick to note that this will have the fox guarding the hen house.

Despite the outward signs of cooperation from the television interests, there is a familiar rumbling in the wings: the government plan would mandate V-chip technology in the manufacture of all televisions with 13-inch or larger screens. Civil liberties groups and networks are already hinting that such a plan had better be voluntary, because any mandatory regulations would surely prompt litigation alleging a violation of First Amendment rights. Although the V-chip is not a panacea, if it does come into use, it should help caring parents select more suitable programming for their children.

More should and could be done by the movie moguls and television tycoons to tame media violence. A good start would be for writers and directors to exercise creativity, self-restraint, and professionalism. This should lead to better stories, plots with greater substance, worthwhile social messages, and a long overdue show of social responsibility. But this is likely just Alice in Wonderland wistfulness, because mercenary interests will balk at taming the violence since their principal yardstick is Nielsen TV ratings and box office profits, not social responsibility and taste.

Although strongly suggested by scientific research, no cause-and-effect relationship between violence in entertainment and crime can be irrefutably proven. And, owing to the intangible nature of the electronic media, it likely never will be. Nevertheless, the police deal with the unsolicited, violent by-products of the entertainment industry. They need relief from the violence, and should clamor for it. If there is progress on no other front in the reduction of media violence, the police themselves should act. By flexing their collective muscle through employee organizations, such as successfully squelching "Cop Killer," police officers may create uncomfortable publicity for the purveyors of violence, while spearheading national economic sanctions against sponsors who allow producers to overdo violent and anti-police programs.

Despite the negative press officers sometimes receive, by and large the public trusts and supports its police. Any special interest that has the trust of the public has immense power. Police organizations should use this public trust and power to lobby for worthwhile causes that benefit society.

Survivor Benefits

The most significant survivor benefit measure ever passed at the federal level of government was the Public Safety Officer Benefits Act of 1976, spelled out in Section 42 U.S.C. 3796, et. seq. This measure was initially proposed in 1971 to provide $50,000 to survivors of police officers murdered in the line of duty, irrespective of what level of government they served. It took five years and a host of versions, before an Act of such high merit was passed by the United States Congress.

The law is administered by the Public Safety Officers' Benefits Program, Bureau of Justice Assistance (BJA), 633 Indiana Avenue NW, Washington, D.C. The telephone number is: 202-307-0635. The FAX number is: 202-514-5956. Eligible survivors or disability claimants may file claims directly with the BJA at the address listed above or through the public safety agency, organization, or unit in which the victim officer served. The BJA is prepared to assist survivors or claimants with questions they may have about eligibility, procedures, and forms.

The Public Safety Officer Benefit Act is regularly being fine-tuned. A major change, effective after June 1, 1988, called for a payment of $100,000 in the case of deaths occurring after that date. And as of October, 1988, the benefit is adjusted each year on October 1 to reflect the percentage of change in the Consumer Price Index. Hence, for fiscal year 1997, the benefit is $138,461. Another change since the original Act was passed in 1976 allows that deaths attributable to stress or exertion encountered in the course of duty may fall under the Act's provisions.

It is time for each state to pass meaningful survivor benefits legislation to supplement the federal measure. While some states have done so, others should follow. Ideally, state benefit packages should include medical care, compensation for temporary, total, and permanent disability, and monthly compensation for an officer's survivors. Funds should also be mandated so that the surviving children of a slain public safety officer may be educated beyond high school.

In many places across America, public spirited citizens have formed associations to provide some financial security for survivors of officers killed in the line of duty. These groups, called Hundred Clubs, were organized in Detroit in 1952 following the murder of an officer there. Hundred Clubs cannot fill the financial gap between a survivor's dollar needs and benefits which inure to him or her through the spouse's employer, but the organization tries to ease the burden by making a lump sum payment to help with immediate and near-range expenses. Hundred Clubs representatives have lobbied ardently in favor of death benefits legislation in the District of Columbia, as well as in state houses across the nation. Ordway P. Burden is President of the Law Enforcement Assistance Foundation, Inc., and is a Hundred Clubs founder. He may be reached at: 250 E. 87th Street, #31-G, New York, NY 10128-3115. Phone: 212-534-8396. FAX: 212-348-4065.

While neither a countermeasure, nor a legislative proposal as such, it is significant that the National Law Enforcement Policy Center, a unit of the International Association of Chiefs of Police, has prepared a model policy which addresses line-of-duty deaths. It provides agencies with guidance about how they may handle a tragic event of this nature as efficiently and graciously as possible. The model policy sets out guidelines which are appropriate to helping and supporting the deceased member's survivors because the family of an officer who is fatally injured needs help of a special sort, such as assistance of varying kinds for the widow or widower about the problems to be faced as a survivor. For example, there are predictable legal and technical problems which will suddenly come into the life of a surviving mate. Some of these entanglements are very complicated; all are very emotional and come at a time when survivors may not be thinking clearly. In addition, a cogent, timely article which appeared in the May, 1996, issue of *The Police Chief* relates what faced Roseville, California, Police Chief Thomas H. Simms in the wake of a line-of-duty death in his force. Chief Simms, in his telling article, identifies the event as "... the toughest, most meaningful challenge of your professional career. ..."

While a line-of-duty death will touch only a few of the nation's 18,000 police departments, the eventualities should be frankly anticipated by every force and family. The IACP's model policy, described above, is in place to help departments cope. At the same time, young police couples should not postpone discussing what arrangements should be made in the event of death. Also, senior couples must be certain that arrangements made earlier are still timely. Moreover, it is urgent that important personal records are kept and are readily accessible, such as insurance papers, birth and marriage certificates, financial and banking papers, and wills. Wills must not only be in order, but updated and accessible, too. Custodian accounts, pension board and social security information, fringe benefit agreements, veterans' benefits, and police association or union records are examples of important documents which need to be at hand. So should income tax records and any contracts and school transcripts as well as safety deposit box keys, the number and combination of the officer's departmental locker, and keys to any other equipment repositories or offices.

It would be very helpful if the department made a competent financial advisor available to the survivor at this troubled time. This person's services may be provided as a benefit of union or police association membership, or perhaps through the jurisdiction's personnel department. The force should urge officers to maintain never-ending orderliness in their personal affairs, too.

Concerns of Police Survivors, Inc., is an organization highly relevant to those who have suffered the death of a public safety employee. Founded in 1982, the organization is active on many fronts. One of its principal contributions is its 3-day training seminar, "The Trauma of Law Enforcement Death," in which participants are expected to gain valuable knowledge that will help assure their agencies' ability to respond effectively in the event of an officer's death.

Another significant contribution of Concerns of Police Survivors, Inc., is its handbook, *Support Services to Surviving Families of Line-of Duty Death*. The handbook has proven invaluable to many families and police departments who suddenly are confronted with a personal calamity of unimaginable dimension. C.O.P.S. Inc., may be reached at P.O. Box 3199, Camdenton, Mo., 65020. The telephone number is: 573-346-4911. FAX: 573-346-1414.

Chapter 11

A FERTILE ARENA FOR RESEARCH

As the President's Commission on Law Enforcement and Administration of Justice so aptly observed, "... the greatest need is the need to know ..." much more about the American justice system. Research, the key to knowing much more about all sorts of things, is sorely needed in order to get a better handle on the anatomy of attacks on police. Surprisingly little research has been done in this specific arena in spite of the epidemic nature of assaults on police.

Since 1960, the only national information about the assault and murder of police has been the annual statistics provided by the Federal Bureau of Investigation, which are shown in Table 1.1. Though useful because they give a sense of how extensive the problem of cop fighting is, the FBI data are merely numbers which are limited in scope and are underreported. Moreover, they lack analyses, and have never purported to address the specific questions pertaining to murders and assaults which must be researched in any thorough study of violence against law enforcement officers.

Over the years, many reports about cop fighting have been written by law enforcement officials and published in police journals of varying respectability. In addition, from time to time, journalists have prepared features on the issue which were published in news magazines or op-ed sections of newspapers. These were usually highly impressionistic reports, based on day-to-day observations by a police officer or an investigative writer, and were not research. They focused on specific operational aspects of attacks on police and provided no systematic treatment of the many factors surrounding assault and murder incidents. Impressionistic essays continue to be published, some of which feature the drama and emotion linked to a single incident, but they show little that is new while underscoring the vexing problem of cop fighting and police murders.

Despite the urgency of the assault and murder problem, little of a technical and analytical nature was known about assaults on police and their murders until mid-1974. At that time, a report stemming from a 20-month study on the subject, under sponsorship of a grant from the U.S. Department of Justice, was published by the Bureau of Government Research at the University of Oklahoma. This research subjected violence against police to a deliberate, broadly-based and systematic integrative analysis. The project, called The Police Assaults Study, had as its data base information assembled during 1973 from 37 municipal law enforcement agencies in the five southwestern states. The data base totaled over 1,100 accounts of assaults on officers, ranging from hundreds of encounters where no injuries were suffered, to one which resulted in the murder of an officer. From these, the research team compiled a descriptive profile of assaults with three main categories of information: (1) officer characteristics; (2) assailant characteristics; and (3) the circumstances of the assault itself. Under officer characteristics, the analysis of height, build, race, rank, age, length of service, and training yielded little to indicate that any particular kind of police officer is more likely than others to be attacked. The traditional belief that "little" police officers attract more trouble than "big" ones was not borne out by the data.

Assailant characteristics also indicated that short people, although represented among assailants, are not more likely to assault police officers than taller ones. Women were less likely to commit assaults than men. Nonwhites were not more likely to assault police than whites. The average age of assailants was 28.2 years; the under-18 age group represented a surprisingly low percentage. Unemployed persons were more likely to commit assaults than people in a job, and persons of lower socioeconomic status constituted a disproportionately large percentage. Alcohol or other drug use immediately prior to the assault was identified as a highly salient factor among those attacking officers.

The assault incident itself, about which complex data were assembled, yielded useful information: the majority of assaults occurred during the hours of darkness, the leisure and drinking hours. The greatest frequency was during July, and over one-third were on streets or highways, many coming while an officer was attempting an arrest.

The next highest scene was the private residence, confirming that the domestic dispute is a prime setting for assaults on police. Ten percent took place during charging or detention, which marked the jail as a far more hazardous site than most people realize, as was underscored in Chapter 8. Officers on auto patrol, but who were going about their duties while on foot, were by far the most often assaulted. The presence of more than one officer by no means reduced the likelihood of assault: in 87.6 percent of the cases, more than one lawman was there. Active physical support by civilian bystanders was given three times as often to police as to assailants, but in 60 percent of cases civilian witnesses remained passive or neutral. In over half the assaults the officer was uninjured. A firearm was used in only 2.2 percent of the assaults. These, and many more interesting points, with lessons both for operational and training purposes, came out of the police assaults study.

The Oklahoma research staff sub-contracted with the International Association of Chiefs of Police to evaluate the murders of officers stemming from ambush attacks and robberies in progress. The IACP published two risk reduction manuals: *Ambush Attacks* and *Robbery Events*. Both proved to be useful reports which identified means of coping with these vicious attacks primarily by improving police field procedures, equipment and training.

There has not been much more research about attacks on police since the Oklahoma study, in spite of the urgent nature of the issue. A few prominent scholars have done some writing but, for the most part, their research has not been of an integrative nature and, hence, did not include conclusions of the nature made by the police assaults study.

On two occasions, *The Annals* of the American Academy of Political and Social Science have highlighted articles about the police and violence. In 1966, an entire issue of *The Annals*, edited by Dr. Thorsten Sellin, included 14 such articles, most of which addressed the psychological and sociological aspects of violent behavior. Only one article dealt with aggressive crimes, and its writer concluded that the scarcity of statistics prevented identification of trends in this area. None of the 14 articles was precisely on point relative to police officer victimization.

In 1980, *The Annals* filled 156 or its 211-page November issue with 14 more articles, many of which related to the police. In an article introducing this issue of *The Annals*, Dr. Lawrence W. Sherman acknowledges that little is known about violence against the police:

> As little as we know about how . . . to reduce civic violence, we know even less about how to reduce violence against the police. The ignorance is sur-

prising given the great official attention and funding the issue has received. . . . Millions of dollars have . . . been spent on supporting the widows, but barely any federal funds have been spent on research to discover how to prevent such deaths. Nor have social scientists . . . initiated much of their own research on violence against the police.

The writers of the 156 pages addressed three major themes: (1) police against violence; (2) violence against police; and (3) violence by police. The writers concluded that while police and violence are central to the American concept of government, four questions linger: (1) how can the police act more effectively and justly against violence in society? (2) how can the violence against police be better understood, and then reduced? (3) what accounts for the wide variation in police use of violence? and (4) what can be learned from that variation to reduce police violence to the lowest possible level?

Other researchers have been heard. In 1981, Professor David Lester of Stockton State College in New Jersey, presented a paper before the Academy of Criminal Justice Sciences. Professor Lester calculated the death rates of police officers murdered from 1971 to 1978 in the largest American cities, and then correlated the data with a host of other crime, suicide, geographical, and climatic conditions, city by city. Among other things, he noted that a unique feature of law enforcement as a career is that its personnel have the highest risk of fatality from murder, as contrasted to occupational fatality rates from accidental death.

In 1982, three consecutive issues of *The Journal of Police Science and Administration* addressed "Violence and the Police: An Analysis of Robbery-Related Assault Incidents." Dr. James J. Fyfe of the American University noted that Dr. C. Kenneth Meyer, the principal author of the feature, and his colleagues have taken the detailed information about robberies, analyzed it, and related the findings to the situations that account for most of the serious injuries and murders of police. Fyfe wrote that ". . . they have made a very important contribution to our knowledge about police-citizen violence . . ."

In a 1984 article, Professor David N. Konstantin found that the majority of incidents in which an officer was murdered was one which the officer, rather than a citizen, initiated. Konstantin suggested that officers were inadequately prepared when they initiated contacts and unknowingly placed themselves in dangerous situations. He advised that police training should focus not only on citizen-initiated routine activities, but also on the necessity to carefully approach police-involved situations. He also found that officer deaths stemming from domestic disputes were not so many as is popularly believed, adding that the greatest category of lives lost were while attempting other arrests. Konstantin concluded his feature by declaring that ". . . there exists a real and continuing need for analysis of the killings to . . . effectively address contemporary hazards."

Five informative publications since 1985 warrant recognition. One, published in 1988, reports on assaults on personnel of the Baltimore County Police Department during the three-year period 1984 - 1986. As the report drew to conclusion, the following observation was made:

> . . . We know who was involved, where the event occurred, and at what time, but we need to know more about what happened and why it occurred in order to prevent future violence from taking place. The interaction between the police and the offender is crucial to that understanding.

Professor Robert Little and Charlotte, North Carolina, Officer Max Boylen wrote two articles which were published in 1990. One, which appeared in the London-based *Police Journal*, addressed fatal assaults on United States law enforcement officers. Their other article, which appeared in *The Journal of Police Science and Administration*, reports on the types of firearms police officers are likely to encounter during the course of their work. One of the means they used to assess the threat was innovative: they recorded the annual number and exact nature of weapons confiscated by police.

An article by Dr. Lawrence Sherman and four others looked closely at officers who were murdered in drug-related situations from 1972 to 1988. It was published by the Crime Control Institute of Washington, D.C. This valuable article observed that:

> The good news about the findings is that so few officers have been killed, relative to the enormous numbers of drug enforcement situations. The bad news is that the numbers of deaths have been increasing—as a proportion of all deaths since 1985, and in total deaths in 1988.

In late 1992, the FBI's Uniform Crime Reports Section published a 61-page monograph which studied selected felonious killings of police officers. This publication marks the first time that the FBI has taken its extensive data on police deaths and subjected them to serious research. The publication reports on a comprehensive, extensive project which, in an integrative approach, examined the police officers, offenders, and the situations which brought them together into events with fatal consequences for police. For years, the need for such an integrative approach has been stressed by various researchers, but such research has been hindered by difficulties in collecting adequate data, particularly in relation to the psychology of the offender. The FBI study is an important one which offers the law enforcement community information that can assist individual agencies in addressing survival training needs.

While scholars have raised questions relevant to attacks on police, they have provided few answers. The last paragraph of *The Annals'* 14th article most lucidly describes the dilemma of research in this complicated sector:

> Shootings are a part of the routine unpredictability of police work. They will occur, but the practical circumstances surrounding their occurrence will vary and therefore so will their meaning. Researchers have sought to code and compare certain features of police shootings such that a descriptive and —ideally—explanatory model or theory can be built . . . it must be remembered that for the police officer such a theory will have no essential application for it will always be superficial to the contextually embedded phenomenon it attempts to understand. . . . Though we can never underestimate the potential solace served by a theory, it is, in the end, something that is imposed. Police shootings, as incidents to be studied for the light they cast on various theories of police behavior, will therefore never be clearly understood.

In spite of the publications identified above, and a few others, there remains a massive need for research and writing about attacks on police. The subject begs for investigation of an applied sort, with findings being translated into action programs directed toward casualty reduction. This means there must be significant fiscal resources earmarked for research of this nature.

Dollars could be committed to uniquely qualified universities or foundations to conduct the research. Furthermore, there are governmental units specifically studying violence which could be assigned an appropriate, precise role in such deliberations. One of these is the Violence Epidemiology Branch of the Center for Health Promotion and Education, Centers for Disease Control in Atlanta, Georgia. It may be an appropriate base for research, as it does epidemiological research on violence related to rape, homicide, suicide, child abuse, child neglect, and spouse abuse, but not about attacks on police. Another possible government unit to conduct research about attacks on police is the National Center for the Analysis of Violent Crime (NCAVC), headquartered in Quantico, Virginia, at the FBI's National Academy. The NCAVC, developed in 1984, is collecting data about and analyzing serial murders, forcible rapes, arsons, and other targeted crimes. The Uniform Crime Reports Section, assisted as it was in 1992 by the Behavioral Science Services Unit at the FBI Academy, may be inspired to do additional research.

Another potential base for research about cop killings is the Mental Health branch of the United States Department of Health and Human Services. A fourth prospect, depending upon the level and nature of its funding and its mission, is the National Institute of Justice within the U.S. Department of Justice. In addition, there appears to be no valid reason why joint funds from the National Centers for Disease Control and the Mental Health interests could not be parlayed with U.S. Department of Justice funds and used, if the scope of research were of sufficient breadth, which it easily could be. Finally, private foundations should be encouraged to participate, since follow-on research in the area of police casualties is so urgent and the potential pay-off from applied research is so great.

In any case, with nearly two million assaults on officers and 3,367 officers murdered over the 50 years between 1945 - 1994, it is timely for important branches of the major U.S. Cabinet-level departments to initiate research about this epidemic. The FBI monograph concisely summarizes the rational for more research:

> Given the extraordinary pressure of decision-making in law enforcement, combined with a mix of deadly factors such as disordered personalities of the offenders, misperception of imminent threats, and possible procedural miscues that are characteristic of these incidents, it is clear that further research on all aspects of law enforcement safety is needed.

Chapter 12

CONCLUSION

American police officers, and policing as an institution, will survive the epidemic of attacks on and murders of police. Both men and women officers of the system, and the system itself, have proven resilient, showing impressive will and ability to bounce back. Their character seems aptly described by the words of an old, anonymous Scottish ballad, a tribute to the come-back powers of warriors led by a chief of great courage:

> "Ffight on my men," says Sir Andrew Bartton,
> "I am hurt, but I am not slaine;
> I'le lay me downe and bleed a-while,
> and then I'le rise and ffight againe."

Persistent, prolonged and uncurbed attacks on police could conceivably precipitate unwelcome suppressive countermeasures foreign to a free society. Therefore, it is important that assaults on police be reduced, but within the framework of comprehensive programs which specify carefully reasoned responses. Hopefully, these programs will lessen the number of assaulted police and be evidence of America's commitment to the preservation of life.

In conclusion, the bottom line is this: while the implementation of various lifesaving measures is important to reducing casualties, the most critical area is the six inches between the ears of each officer!

BIBLIOGRAPHY

Ardrey, R., *Territorial Imperative*. New York: Antheneum Press, 1966.

Brooks, P. R., ...*Officer Down, Code Three.*. Motorola Teleprograms, Inc., 1975.

Chapman, S. G.; Hale, C. D.; Meyer, C. Kenneth; Swanson, Cheryl G.; & Morrison, P. M., *Perspectives on Police Assaults in the South Central United States*. vols. I, II, and III and *Operations Research Manual*. Norman, OK: University of Oklahoma, Office of Research Administration, 1974.

Cheek, J. C. & Lesce, T., Plainclothes and Off-Duty Officer Survival. Springfield, IL: Charles C Thomas, Publisher, 1988.

Concerns of Police Survivors, Inc., *Support Services to Surviving Families of Line-of Duty Death*: A Public Safety Agency Handbook. Camdenton, MO: C.O.P.S., Inc., March, 1994.

Davis, E. F. & Pinizzotto, A. J., Above and Beyond the Call of Duty: Preventing Off-duty Officer Deaths, *The FBI Law Enforcement Bulletin*, vol. 65, no. 4, April 1996, 1-5.

Fast, J., *Body Language*. New York: Pocket Books, 1970.

Federal Bureau of Investigation, Uniform Crime Reports, *Law Enforcement Officers Killed and Assaulted* for years 1972 through 1994. Washington, D. C.: Federal Bureau of Investigation.

Federal Bureau of Investigation, Uniform Crime Reports, *Crime in the United States - Uniform Crime Reports* for years 1960 through 1984. Washington, D.C.: Federal Bureau of Investigation.

Fleck, T., Police Dogs and the Law, *Longline*, vol. 96, no. 1, 1996, 15-16.

Hoover, J. E., Message From the Director, *FBI Law Enforcement Bulletin*, vol. 37, no. 9, September 1967, 1.

International Association of Chiefs of Police, *Robbery Incidents: A Risk Reduction Manual*. Gaithersburg, MD: The Police Weapons Center, 1974.

International Association of Chiefs of Police, *Murder in America: Recommendations from the IACP Murder Summit*. Alexandria, VA: IACP, May 1995.

International Association of Chiefs of Police, *Ambush Attacks: A Risk Reduction Manual for Police*. Gaithersburg, MD: The Police Weapons Center, 1974.

Kelley, C. M., Message From the Director, *FBI Law Enforcement Bulletin*, vol. 43, no. 2, February 1974, 1.

Konstantin, D. N., Homicides of American Law Enforcement Officers, 1978-1980, *Justice Quarterly*, vol. 1, no. 1, 1984, 29-45.

Lester, D., The Police As Victims: Analyses of Murdered Police Officers, a paper presented before the Academy of Criminal Justice Sciences at Philadelphia, PA, 1981.

Little, R. & Boylen, M., Cop-Killing–A Descriptive Analysis of the Problem, *Police Studies*, vol. 7, 1984, 68-76.

Little, R. & Boylen, M., Fatal Assaults on United States Law Enforcement Officers, *Police Journal*, vol. 63, no. 1, 1990, 61-77.

Meyer, C. K. et al., *Ambush-Related Assaults on Police: Violence at the Street Level*. Springfield, IL: Charles C Thomas, Publisher, 1986.

Meyer, C. K. et al., Violence and the Police: The Special Case of the Police Assailant, *The Journal of Police Science and Administration*, vol. 7, no. 2, 1979, 161-171.

Meyer, C. K. et al., *Violence and the Police: An Analysis of Robbery-Related Assault Incidents*. Norman, OK: Bureau of Government Research, 1983.

Rachlin, H., Police Officer Deaths: Killed in the Line of Duty, *Law and Order*, vol. 42, no. 9, September 1994, 129-172.

Remsberg, C., *The Tactical Edge: Surviving High-Risk Patrol*. Northbrook, IL: Calibre Press, 1986.

Remsberg, C., et al., *Street Survival: Tactics for Armed Encounters*. Northbrook, IL: Calibre Press, 1980.

Remsberg, C., *Tactics for Criminal Patrol*. Northbrook, IL: Calibre Press, 1995.

Sanders, D. L., 21st-Century Issues for Women in Policing, *The Police Chief*, vol 63, no. 1, January 1997, 6.

Sherman, L. W., et al., *Police Murdered in Drug-Related Situations, 1972-1988*. Washington, D.C.: Crime Control Institute, 1989.

Sherman, L. W., ed., The Police and Violence, *The Annals*, vol. 452, November 1980, 1-150.

Simms, T. H., Your Worst Nightmare Has Just Come True, *The Police Chief*, vol. 63, May 1996, 26-33.

Thompson, G. J., & Jenkins, J. B., *Verbal Judo: The Gentle Art of Persuasion*. New York: W. Morrow, 1993.

Thompson, G. J., *Verbal Judo: Words for Street Survival*. Springfield, IL: Charles C Thomas, Publisher, 1983.

Uchida, C. D., & Brookes, L. W., *Violence Against the Police: Assaults on Baltimore County Police, 1984-1986 Final Report*. College Park, MD: University of Maryland Institute of Criminal Justice and Criminology, 1988.

United States Department of Justice, Federal Bureau of Investigation, *Killed in the Line of Duty: A Study of Selected Felonious Killings of Law Enforcement Officers*. Washington, D.C.: September 1992.

Walters, S. B., *Principles of Kinesic Interview and Interrogation*. Boca Raton, FL: CRC Press, 1996.

Wilbanks, W., Punishing Cop-Killers: An Historical Perspective, a paper presented before the Academy of Criminal Justice Sciences at Pittsburgh, PA, 1992.

Wilson, L. A., *A Situational Analysis of Police Assaults*. Norman, OK: The University of Oklahoma, a dissertation submitted to the Graduate Faculty, 1990.

INDEX

A
Academy of Criminal Justice Sciences, 186
Accidental death of police, 12, 42
Alcohol, chemical dependency, 53-54, 156, 170-174
    a factor in police murder, 53, 156, 172
    cause of attacks on police, 31, 53-55, 115, 140, 184
Alcoholics Anonymous (AA), 173
Alfred P. Murrah Federal Office Building, ix, 27, 42, 116, 177
Alternatives to incarceration, 141, 144-145
Altus, Oklahoma, 38
American Psychological Association, 175
American Society of Law Enforcement Trainers, 98
Ambush attacks, 20, 25, 88, 92, 114-115, 150, 152, 185
    and civil disorder, 20, 26
    number of, 25-26
Anderson, Dennis, 98
Annals of the American Academy of Political and Social Science, 185, 188
Ardmore, Oklahoma, 21-22, 28, 38, 52, 61, 67
Ardrey, Robert, 80
Arraignment, 67
Arrests/dismissed charges, 68-69
Assaults on police, v, 5, 7
    failure to report, 7, 8
    forms used by FBI for reporting, 8-11
Auxiliary police, 107-108

B
Bail, 49, 66-67
Baltimore County Police Department, 187
Baltimore, Maryland, 129
Body armor, 130-131
    helmets, 132-133
Body language, 80-82, 89
Boylen, Officer Max, 187
Branch Davidian compound, 116, 150
Bratt, Larry, 176
Brooks, Pierce R., xi, 93, 105
Burden, Ordway P., 181
Burglary, 21, 57, 91
    as a non-violent offense, 57
    in progress, 22, 115, 126
    pursuing suspects in, 57

C
Caddo, Oklahoma, 19
Calibre Press, 98
Canadian Police Information System (CPIC), 129
Canine/officer teams, 101, 114-117, 133, 144, 148
Capital punishment, 60-61, 65, 72. 161-164
Carelessness/complacency, vi, x, 24, 37, 90 93, 101, 105, 140, 146, 171
Casualties, no acceptable level of, vi
Clearance rate for police killings, 19-20
Communication systems, 122-130
    body transmitters, 146
    cellular phones, 129
    computerized information systems, 125-127, 129-130
    computers, 122-127, 129-130, 166
    electronic car locators, 126-127
    E-mail, 148
    radio, dispatch, 122-124
    radio, personal, 127
    regional, 124
    telephones, 122-125
    311 - nonemergency number, 129
    E-911 - emergency number, 128
    911 - emergency number, 124, 127-129
Community policing, 109-110

Concerns of Police Survivors, Inc. (COPS), 182
Congressional Office of Technology Assessment, 171
Con talk, 82-86
"Cop Killer", 176, 178-179
"CopNet", 84
Corrections, 82-86, 137-144
   employees in, 82, 84-85, 137
   lexicographer, 84
Countersurveillance, 149
Crime Control Institute of Washington, D.C., 187
Cults, 149-151
Cultures, diverse, 81-82

D

Delay, 63-64, 157
Drug Awareness Resistance Education (DARE), 172
Drug dealers, 152
Drug laboratories, vi, 148
Drug raids, 43, 147, 151-152
Drugs and drug abuse, 118-119, 143, 145-148, 170-174
Dynamic Striking Techniques, 90

E

Emergency response team (ERT), 110, 134
Enid, Oklahoma, 32
Equipment, protective, 121-136, 160
Evans, John, 84
Explorer scouts, 108

F

Fast, Julius, 80
Federal Aviation Administration regulations, 113
Federal Bureau of Investigation (FBI), 5, 15, 20-21, 25, 43, 79, 129-130, 135, 151, 183, 187-189
   Crime in the United States: Uniform Crime Reports, 7, 15
   crime reporting programs, 7, 57
   index offenses, 7, 57
   Law Enforcement Bulletin, 33, 89, 157
   law enforcement officers killed, 6, 7
   Law Enforcement Officers Killed and Assaulted, 15
National Academy, 189
National Crime Information Center (NCIC), 129-130
Federal Communications Commission, 129, 178
Female police, x, 41-43
Field procedures, 94, 102, 109-113
Films and video cassettes, 98
Fingerprints, 156
Firearms, 33, 156-161
   handguns, 33-35
   retention, 35, 43, 68, 112
   rifles, 33, 35
   shotguns, 33, 35
Firearms training simulation (FATS), 100 101
Flavor-Fav, 176
Foreword looking infrared (FLIR), 135
Fort Smith, Arkansas, 32
Freemen, 151
Fyfe, Dr. James J., 186

G

Games/prison, 82-86
Gansta rap, 175-176, 178
Gore, Tipper, 176, 178
Gustafson Lake, Canada standoff, 117

H

Highway patrol, 19, 27-28, 32, 38, 46-47, 61, 126
Hoover, J. Edgar, 33, 92, 106, 157-159
Hundred Clubs, 181

I

Ice-T, 176, 178
Institute of Police Technology and Management, 98
Intelligence, 151
International Association of Chiefs of Police (IACP), 104, 155, 168, 181, 185
   National Law Enforcement Policy Center, 104, 181
   Violence in America Summit, 1994, 155-156
International Association of Law Enforcement Firearms Instructors, 98
Internet, 84-85, 148

J

Jails, 137-144
  consolidation of, 141-142
  contraband in, 142-144
  danger in, 137-141, 185
  overcrowding, 139
  security, 115, 144
  standards, 138, 141
Journal of Police Science and Administration, 186-187

K

Kansas City, 129
  Automated Law Enforcement Response Team (ALERT), 129-130
Kelley, Clarence M., 92
Kevlar, 131
Kinesics, 80-82
King, Jr., Dr. Martin Luther, 116
Konstantin, Professor David N., 186-187

L

Law Enforcement Assistance Administration (LEAA), 131
Law Enforcement Memorial Association, 3, 42
Lawton, Oklahoma, 32
Legislation, 155-168, 180
  armor-piercing ammunition, 159-160
  asset forfeiture, 152
  autopsy, 164-166
  Brady Handgun Violence Prevention Act of 1994, 160-161
  capital punishment, 161-164
  conceal and carry laws, 161
  Federal Motor Vehicle Safety Standards (FMVSS), 168
  firearms control, 156-161
  Gun Control Act of 1968, 159, 161
  license plate requirements, reflectorization, 166-168
  liquor laws, 172
  magazine ammunition limit, 160-161
  mandated minimum sentences, 161
  medical examiner system, 165
  National Bank Robbery Act, 156
  National Firearms Act of 1934, 159
  nontransparent or reflective glass, tinting, 168
  Omnibus Crime Control and Safe Streets Act of 1968, 132, 159
  Public Safety Officer Benefits Act of 1976, 180
  Speedy Trial Act, 157
  Sullivan Law of 1911, 158
Lester, Professor David, 186
Little, Professor Robert, 187
Los Angeles, 43, 94, 176

M

McVeigh, Timothy, 27, 177
Manslaughter, 70-71
Manuals, procedural, 38, 104, 140
Mental health facilities, 54, 69, 93
Mentally disturbed persons, 27, 51, 55, 89, 93, 138
Meyer, Dr. C. Kenneth, 186
Misidentification of police, 43, 147-148
Mobile home, trailer, 149, 152-154
Moonlighting, 106-107
Murder of police (see police deaths)
Murderers, police, 48-61
  age range of, 49, 51
  alcohol and drug use, 53-54
  birthplace, 50
  criminal profiles of, 54-59
  educational achievement, 52
  escapees, 19, 49, 51, 53-54, 57, 61, 115, 137-138, 140, 142-143
  frequency of prior convictions, 59-61
  gender and race, 49-50
  occupation and employment, 53
  parole/probation, 49, 58
  prior arrests, 55-56, 59
  representation by counsel, 65-66
MTV, 176

N

National Law Enforcement Officers Memorial Fund, 3, 42
National Center for the Analysis of Violent Crime (NCAVC), 189
National Commission on the Causes and Prevention of Violence, 1968, 175
National Institute of Corrections, 138
National Institute of Mental Health, 175
National Rifle Association, 161
Night vision devices, 134-135

Norman, Oklahoma, vii, ix, 32, 141

O

"...*Officer Down, Code Three.*", xi, 93
Officer field survival, 87-88
Oklahoma City Police Department, 18, 32, 57, 67, 69
Oklahoma Court of Criminal Appeals, 64, 67, 71, 163
Oklahoma Department of Corrections, 15
Oklahoma Office of the State Medical Examiner, 15
Oklahoma State Bureau of Investigation, 15
Oklahoma State Historical Society, 15
Oswald, Lee Harvey, 159

P

Parent Music Research Center (PMRC), 176, 178
Parent Teacher Association (PTA), 176, 178
Patrols, 37-39, 166-167, 185
  mandating two-officer, 38
  one- vs. two-officer, 22, 27, 37-39, 185
Penitentiaries, 61, 83, 137
Persuasion, vii, 88-90
Physical fitness programs, 108, 115
Plea bargaining, 65
Police Assaults Study, vii, 48, 184-185
Police Chief, 181
Police deaths
  activity performed when murdered, 20-28
  by age range, 44-46
  attempting arrests, 20, 23
  birthplace, 44
  by day of the week, 28-30
  daylight or darkness, 31-32, 37
  distance between victim and murderer, 35-36
  drug related matters, 21, 146
  educational achievement, 48
  family quarrels/domestic disturbances, 21, 91, 99, 101, 114, 156, 184
  gender and race, 41-43
  geography of, 44
  interval between, 17-19
  marital status, 47
  military experience, 44, 48
  by month, 28-29
  murdered with own weapon, 35
  number of, 6, 12, 35, 101, 189
  preventable, 37, 73-74, 77, 131, 142, 145, 155, 157, 159, 165
  prior police experience, 47
  suspicious circumstances, persons, 24
  time of day, 28-32
  by type of weapon, 33
Police Control and Restraining Techniques, 90
Police Journal (London), 187
President's Commission on Law Enforcement and Administration of Justice, viii, 77, 183
Principles of Kinesic Interview and Interrogation, 80
Prisoners, 21, 23-24, 99, 110-113, 138, 140, 142-143
  handcuffing, 23-24, 111-113, 140
  searching, 23-24, 111, 143
  transporting, 20-21, 23, 99, 111-113, 138, 142

R

Ray, James Earl, 116
Recreational vehicles (RVs), 116, 149, 152-154
Remsberg, Charles, xi, 98
Research, 74, 164, 183-189
Robberies in progress, 21-22, 115, 185
Royal Canadian Mounted Police, 79, 114, 117, 135, 148, 150

S

"Saturday night specials", 159
Sellin, Dr. Thorsten, 185
Sentencing, 70-72, 163
  appeals, 69
  death penalty, 71-72, 163
  time from arrest to, 64, 70
Sequoyah County, Oklahoma, 32
Sergeants/first level supervisors, 103, 105, 109
Sherman, Dr. Lawrence W., 185, 187
Sherron, Sheriff James, 3
Simms, Chief Thomas H., 181
Sniper attacks, 133, 135, 150
Snoop Doggy Dogg, 176-177
Special detection devices, 133-136
Spencer, Oklahoma, 32, 69

Street Survival, 98
Suicide, by suspect, 19, 22, 54, 61
Survival attitudes, 90
Surviving Edged Weapons (video), 98
Surviving Ground Assaults, 90
Survivor benefits, 180-182
SWAT teams, 110, 134

T
Tactical Edge, 98
Tactics for Criminal Patrol, 98
Tattoos, 82-86
television (*see* violence, television and media)
Territorial Imperative, 80
Terrorists, 92, 116, 135, 150
Thompson, George J., 89
Toxic chemicals, 148-149
Traffic pursuits and stops, 20, 27, 125, 152, 166-167
Training of police officers, 77-102
  behavioral sciences, 79-80
  bulletins, 84, 104
  clear instructional focus, 95
  closed circuit television, 97
  for communications personnel, 122-124
  for corrections personnel, 111-112, 139, 144
  curriculum, 78-79
  effective training strategies, 94-97
  engaged time, 96
  enhancing engagement, 97-98
  field procedures, 87, 118-119, 123
  frequent monitoring/feed back, 96-97, 100
  high expectations, 95
  instruction, 79
  personal defense skills, 88, 90
  simulations, 87, 94, 96, 99-101
  for supervision, 104-105
  time on task, 95-96
  workshops/seminars, 79-80, 98
Trial
  acquittal, 70
  getting to trial, 63
  length of, 69
  preliminary hearings, 68
  (*see also* sentencing)
Tulsa, Oklahoma, 19, 23, 32, 61

Tupac Shakur, 176

U
Undercover law enforcement, 43, 145-151
Urban guerrillas, 149-151
Urban or rural setting, 24, 32, 34, 37, 46-47, 50-52, 59, 61
U.S. Department of Health and Human Services, 188-189
U.S. Department of Health, Education and Welfare, 171
U.S. Department of Justice, 104, 129, 184, 189
  Bureau of Justice Assistance, 104, 180
  Bureau of Justice Statistics, 138, 160
  Law Enforcement Standards Program, 132
  National Institute of Justice, 131, 189
  National Institute of Law Enforcement and Criminal Justice, 112
  National Law Enforcement and Corrections Technology Center (NLECTC), 121
  Office of Science and Technology, 121
U.S. Secret Service, 43
U.S. Supreme Court, 65, 72, 87, 162
  Furman vs. Georgia, 1972, 72, 162
  Gregg vs. Georgia, 1976, 162
  Tennessee vs. Garner, 1985, 87

V
Verbal and non-verbal communication, 88-89
Verbal Judo: the Gentle Art of Persuasion, 90
Verbal Judo: the Martial Art of Mind and Mouth, 89
Video tapes, 84, 89-90, 96-98, 100-101
Violence: television and media, 92, 96-97, 170, 174-180
  cause and effect relationship, 179
  regulation, voluntary rating of shows, 177-179

W
Walters, Stan B., 80
Wambaugh, Joseph, 93
Warrants/execution, 117-118, 147, 149, 160, 164
Washita County, Oklahoma, 18

Washoe County, Nevada, 141
Weapons, 137
    handmade, 137, 143
    highly lethal, 158
    in jails, 137, 140
Wilcott, Corporal Claude, 114